D0013493

W8-BSN-279

PRIMITIVE BEADWORK

At the left is a chain from Luxor, Egypt, of green beads and white shells. The chain at the top is an old Egyptian one. Below is a necklace of deep-red cylindrical beads strung with groups of three shells to represent the Egyptian lotus. In the center hangs the costume of a Sudanese woman. To the right is an Egyptian fly-brush with beaded handle, and below a chain of shells from the Dead Sea strung with dark-blue beads.

How to
Do Beadwork

By

MARY WHITE

Illustrated by the Author

Dover Publications, Inc.,

New York

This Dover edition, first published in 1972, is an
unabridged republication of the work originally
published by Doubleday, Page and Company in
1904.

International Standard Book Number: 0-486-20697-1
Library of Congress Catalog Card Number: 76-183981

Manufactured in the United States of America
Dover Publications, Inc.
180 Varick Street
New York, N. Y. 10014

To Sarah Bartow Johnson

PREFACE

WOMEN come naturally by their love for beads. They inherit it from their "great-great-twenty-seven-times-great-grandmother"—as the fairy tale says.

Close to the first rude implements for household work explorers find bits of shell, turquoise, amber, or lapis lazuli, pierced for stringing; rough and asymmetrical to be sure, but unmistakably beads. Each generation since the time of that very great-grandmother has had the taste for beadwork in a greater or lesser degree, and with the different peoples it has shown itself differently.

With some it has been gorgeous and barbaric; others have wrought with exquisite fineness. Many have only seen in it a personal ornament; while others, like our North American Indian, have used it to beautify alike their household utensils and articles for ceremonial usage. Studying Indian handicrafts, we cannot but recognise the decorative possibilities of beadwork.

Let us see what we can do with it.

GRATEFUL   ACKNOWLEDGMENTS
ARE DUE TO MISS LINA EPPENDORFF
AND MISS ELIZABETH M. STRAIN
FOR THEIR VALUABLE ASSISTANCE

PUBLISHERS'S NOTE

Since Mary White wrote her classic instructions for
beadwork, commercial varieties of beads have changed.
Some beads which she mentions may not be easily
available, except through antique sources: modern bead-
shops, on the other hand, offer many kinds of beads
that were not known in her day. The reader is urged
to use his local resources, while following the author's
exposition of methods and techniques. The projects
presented in this book are not really dependent on
particular kinds of beads, and you can easily make
substitutions to suit your own taste.

CONTENTS

LIST OF ILLUSTRATIONS

LIST OF FIGURES

LIST OF FIGURES—*Continued*

LIST OF FIGURES—*Continued*

LIST OF FIGURES—*Continued*

The Beads and Other Materials

HOW TO DO BEADWORK

CHAPTER I

THE present interest in beadwork undoubt-
edly sprang from our enthusiasm for Indian
handicrafts. From admiring and wishing to
possess baskets wrought with beads, and woven
bead belts and chains, it was a natural and
easy step to copying them. Whether the
special branch of beadwork one wishes to do is
stringing, weaving, knitting, or sewing, the beads
are, of course, the first consideration. Wampum,
the genuine Indian bead, is beautiful and costly.
The wampum used by eastern tribes is long and
cylindrical; in colour ivory-white, black, or purple.
Western wampum, shaped like tiny millstones,
was generally made of clam-shells ground and
drilled by hand. "The aboriginal tool for drilling,
called *dawihai* (from *da win*, to bore, and *hai*, a
stick), was a straight shaft of wood two feet long
and half an inch in diameter at the middle. This

3

the kneeling Indian twirled between the palms of his hands. The drill-point was of jasper or flint and fastened to the shaft by a lashing of hemp coated with pitch. Its origin is beyond tradition.'' Sometimes the Indians fashioned beads of rainbow-coloured abalone shells from the Pacific. The beautiful feather baskets of the Pomos are occasionally enriched by decorations of these beads. Again, in strings of white western wampum one finds a bead of wonderful sky-blue—an exquisite contrast; it is turquoise. These beads, however, are for a fortunate few. Those most of us must be content to possess are the Venetian glass beads, sometimes mistakenly spoken of as Indian, but which are only Indian because they are used by them. Originally these beads were made by hand. A piece of molten glass, while still hot, was pierced, and two boys, holding each an end of the soft but stiffening mass with pincers, ran as fast as possible in opposite directions. The glass, thus drawn to a surprising thinness, still kept its tubelike form: the hole in the middle never closed. It was then cut into tiny lengths as nearly alike as possible. In order to smooth the rough surface of the beads, quantities of them were put into a drum with ashes and turned rapidly for some time. Many of the large beads used for strung chains are made in this country. They come in soft, pale colours of opaque glass and in the same colours in pearly finish. The imitations of baroque pearl can hardly be distinguished from the genuine. In the most perfect of these beads seven coats of pigment are used, and they are filled with a special kind of wax, to give them weight and strength. Other large beads which are used in strung chains are highly coloured and flecked or ornamented with gold or silver. All the colours and combinations we are accustomed to see in Venetian glass are found in these beads. Then there are the seed beads. As one looks at a display of these the masses of shimmering colour make one long for an artist's ability to combine them in things of beauty and use. With the larger, or E beads, one can fashion candle-shades or strung chains. The smaller seed beads range in size from 0 or 1 (as they are called by some dealers), which are the coarsest, to 5–0. The very tiniest beads sold in this country are 5–0 beads, with one side cut, which some dealers call 6–0. They come in small skeins, while the others are generally sold in bunches of eight skeins each. These are the beads for weaving, sewing, knitting, and crocheting. For stringing bead chains dental floss has been found most satisfactory. It may be used with a No. 8 needle. Some persons like the French lace threads for the woof strands in bead-weaving, but an authority on weaving, Miss Eppendorff, prefers the numbered linen thread or Kerr's cotton No. ooo, as the French threads are not entirely reliable as to size. Two spools of the same number will be apt to vary in coarseness. The warp thread should be one-half again as coarse as the woof—No. 60, for example, for warp and No. 90 for woof, with a No. 11 needle when the beads are 4–o. No. 11 needles are also used when No. ooo cotton is chosen for the woof. Often, when the background is to be of another colour than white, it may be advisable to use silk threads—letter D in buttonhole twist for the warp and letter A sewing-silk for the woof, with a No. 12 needle. These may be used with as fine beads as 5–o. In weaving with silk it will be wise to wax both warp and woof threads. In fact, some beadworkers consider this essential with cotton and linen as well. In looms there is a wide choice. On general principles, the simpler the loom the better. Directions for making a practical loom will be found in Chapter III.

In sewing beads on canvas the French canvas will prove finer and more even than any other.

Dealers in artists' materials sell paper marked off into tiny squares which is indispensable if one wishes to make one's own designs. That in which there are sixteen squares to the inch is most useful as nearer the size of the beads. Coloured crayons are also necessary to indicate the colour scheme of each design.

Strung Chains

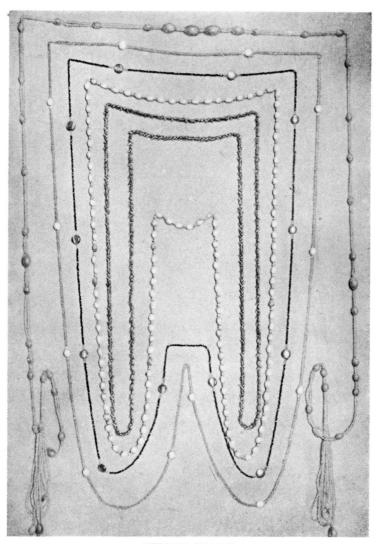

STRUNG CHAINS

The outer chain is of pale-yellow beads. Beside it is a fan chain in crystal, with large blue beads. The next is a black one with green cat-eyes and gold-lined seed beads. Then comes a chain of Job's tears, and within this a string of iridescent shells from Tasmania.

CHAPTER II

THE simplest form of beadwork is, of course, the strung chains. How we loved, as children, to make necklaces of beads or berries! To be allowed to string beads was one of the compensations for a rainy day. It still has a fascination for many of us. Women all over the world have felt the charm, and curious and beautiful are some of the chains they have made. Some have used beads of gold, silver, and semi-precious stones; others beads of shell, amber, and coral; while others still make chains of wooden beads or string beans or berries.

Black-eyed Susans—the tiny scarlet beans tipped with black that tourists bring from Florida —may be pierced and strung and make gay chains. It would seem strange to be able to pick beads for a chain in one's own garden, yet that is what is done by two girls on Long Island. They have a plant on which grow Job's-tears. These tear-shaped seeds, ranging in colour from

pearly white to black (there are brown ones, too),
make attractive muff-chains. The gray ones
are strung with cut-steel seed beads, two between
each of the Job's-tears, and the brown in the
same way, using gold beads to separate them.
But beware, if you raise Job's-tears, of using them
in their natural state. They should be boiled
like chestnuts before stringing, for a tiny grub
is often found in them, and he may at any time
make a meal of the silk on which the beads are
strung, or appear on your muff inopportunely.
Of the seed beads No. o are most used for these
strung chains, with here and there a large Venetian
bead in colours which harmonize with the body
of the chain. The simplest are strung on a single
strand of purse-silk or dental floss about two
yards long. Fan-chains may be shorter—about
a yard and three-quarters.

Other chains are made with two strands, which
are strung for a few inches with seed beads, then
twisted like a rope. A large bead is slipped on, to
hold the twisted strands, and a few inches more
are strung with seed beads. This continues the
whole length of the chain. In finishing, the ends
are tied with a firm knot. When chains are
simply intended for ornament they are finished

with more or less elaborate tassels, and in calcu-
lating the length of silk or floss enough should be
allowed for them. One such chain is made as
follows:

Pale-yellow Chain

Materials Required
2 large pale-yellow oval beads,
10 medium pale-yellow oval beads,
40 small pale-yellow oval beads,
1 bunch pale-yellow crystal seed beads No. o,
7 yards of dental floss,
2 No. 8 needles.

Double a piece of dental floss seven yards
long and on it string two large pale-yellow beads.
These are placed at the middle. String three-
eighths of an inch of seed beads in double strands
with two needles. For the whole length of the
chain the seed beads are thus strung in two
strands, while both threads pass through the
larger beads. One medium oval bead is followed
by three-eighths of an inch of seed beads in two
strands. One small oval bead, two inches of
seed beads, one small oval, one and three-eighths
inches of seed beads, one small oval, one and five-
eighths inches of seed beads, one medium oval
bead, and two inches of seed beads. One small
oval bead is followed by an inch and three-eighths
of seed beads, another small oval bead, two and

a quarter inches of seed beads, a small oval bead, two and three-eighths inches of seed beads, one small oval bead, and three-quarters of an inch of seed beads. Next comes a large oval bead, half an inch of seed beads, one small oval bead, two and an eighth inches of seed beads, one small oval bead, quarter of an inch of seed beads, one small oval, quarter of an inch of seed beads, one small oval, two inches of seed beads, one small oval, and three-quarters of an inch of seed beads. Another large oval bead is followed by three-quarters of an inch of seed beads, one small oval, one and three-quarters inches of seed beads, one small oval, one-quarter of an inch of seed beads. One small oval, one-quarter of an inch of seed beads, one small oval, three-quarters of an inch of seed beads, and one medium oval. This is repeated to make the other side of the chain.

Tassels.—The tassels are formed of five irregular loops and two ends of seed beads. One medium oval bead is strung at the middle of one of the loops, and another at the tip of one of the ends. The other end has a small oval bead at the tip.

Fan-Chain in Black, Green, and Gold

Materials Required
12 green cat-eyes,
96 gold-lined crystal beads No. o,
3 bunches cut-jet beads No. o size,
A piece of black purse-silk two yards and a quarter long,
A No. 8 needle.

The flat round beads known as cat-eyes are particularly beautiful in green. Twelve of these beads combined with gold-lined crystal and cut-jet No. o seed beads make a chain that is as effective as it is simple. The beads are strung on a piece of black purse-silk. This should be two yards and a quarter long, to allow for joining, although the finished chain will be only sixty-eight inches long. Starting at the centre, a green cat-eye is first strung, then four gold-lined crystal beads and four and three-quarters inches of cut-jet seed beads. Four more gold-lined crystal beads are followed by one green cat-eye, four gold-lined crystals, and four and three-quarters inches of cut-jet beads. This order is repeated until six cat-eyes (each having four gold-lined crystal beads on either side of it and separated from the next group by four and three-quarters inches of jet beads) have been strung. Between the sixth cat-eye and the seventh there are five inches of jet beads following four gold-lined crystal beads, and followed by four others. The other side of the chain is strung in the same way, starting at the centre and finishing with the four gold-lined crystal beads which are strung just before the seventh cat-eye. Here the ends are tied securely close to the cat-eye with which the side first strung was finished.

An elaborate chain is made as follows:

Iridescent Pearl and Gold Chain

Materials Required

7 large oval baroque pearls,
4 medium oval baroque pearls,
16 large round pearls,
30 small round pearls,
18 large gold beads,
10 large iridescent cut beads,
About 52 medium iridescent cut beads,
About 118 small iridescent cut beads,
90 flat iridescent cut beads,
4 bunches iridescent seed beads,
1 bunch gold seed beads,
1 spool white purse-silk,
A No. 8 needle.

A piece of white purse-silk about eight yards long is doubled and the chain is started at the centre. One large oval baroque pearl is first strung, then one flat iridescent bead, one large round pearl, one flat iridescent, one large iridescent, one flat iridescent, one gold seed, one large gold bead, one gold seed, one flat iridescent, one large round pearl, one flat iridescent, one small iridescent, one medium iridescent, one flat iridescent, one small iridescent, one flat iridescent, and three and an eighth inches of iridescent seed beads in two strands. One flat iridescent bead is followed by one large gold, one flat iridescent, three gold seeds, one small pearl, three gold seeds, one medium iridescent, three gold seeds, one large round pearl, three gold seeds, one medium iridescent, three gold seeds, one small pearl, one flat iridescent, one large gold, one flat iridescent, and four and a half inches of iridescent seed beads in two strands. One flat iridescent bead is next strung, then one small iridescent, one flat iridescent, one large gold, one flat iridescent, one small pearl, one flat iridescent, one medium iridescent, one flat iridescent, one large oval baroque pearl, one flat iridescent, one large iridescent, one flat iridescent, one small iridescent, one flat iridescent, one medium pearl, one flat iridescent, one small iridescent, one flat iridescent, one large iridescent, one flat iridescent, one large oval baroque pearl, one flat iridescent, one medium iridescent, one flat iridescent, one small pearl, one flat iridescent, one large gold, one flat iridescent, one small iridescent, one flat iridescent, and four and a quarter inches iridescent seed beads in two strands. One flat iridescent bead is followed by one large iridescent, one flat iridescent, one large gold, one flat iridescent, one medium oval pearl, one flat iridescent, one large gold, one flat iridescent, one medium iridescent, one flat iridescent, and three inches of iridescent seed beads in two strings. Next comes a flat iridescent, one small iridescent, one flat iridescent, one large round pearl, one flat iridescent, one small iridescent, one large gold, one small iridescent, one large iridescent, one small iridescent, one large gold, one small iridescent, one flat iridescent, one large round pearl, one flat iridescent, and three and an eighth inches of iridescent seed beads in two strands. One flat iridescent bead is strung, then one small iridescent, one flat iridescent, one large round pearl, three gold seed beads, one medium iridescent, and three gold seed beads. One large round pearl is followed by one flat iridescent, one small iridescent, one flat iridescent, and two and an eighth inches of iridescent seed beads in two strands. A flat iridescent bead comes next, then a medium iridescent, one large iridescent, one flat iridescent, one small pearl, one flat iridescent, one medium iridescent, one large baroque pearl, and a medium iridescent bead. The other half of the chain is strung in the same order.

Tassels.—There are five strands in each tassel, which are strung as follows:

Half an inch of iridescent seed beads, one small iridescent, one medium iridescent, one small iridescent, an inch and a half of iridescent seed beads, one small iridescent, one medium iridescent, one small iridescent, one small pearl, one medium iridescent, one small pearl, and one medium iridescent bead. Three loops of seed beads are made three-quarters of an inch long. The needle is then brought back through the larger beads to where the seed beads began. Here an inch and a half of iridescent seed beads are strung and the needle passes through the larger beads. Half an inch of seed beads completes the strand. The others are strung in the same way.

Daisy Chain

Materials Required
1 spool white sewing-silk, letter A,
No. 12 needles,
1 long bead needle, No. 12,
1 bunch deep-yellow crystal beads No. 2–0,
1 bunch white opaque beads No. 4–0,
1 bunch olive-green crystal beads No. 4–0.

Three needles, one longer than the others, are
threaded with white silk well waxed. The
strands are tied together at one end and the
needles passed through six green crystal beads;
the longer needle also goes through one white

opaque bead, one larger
yellow crystal bead, and
another white opaque
bead. Now pass one of
the other needles (which
we will call No. 2)
through the lower white
bead, thread on three
more white beads, and
bring it up on the right
of the centre through
the upper white bead.
Needle No. 3 follows in
the same way, but on
the left of the centre
(see Fig. 1). Needle
No. 2 is now brought

FIG. 1

down through the beads on the left and up through
the three centre beads. Needle No. 3 comes
down through the three beads on the right and
up through the three centre beads, completing

the daisy. The three strands are then brought through another six green beads and a second daisy is made. The chain is continued in this way for its entire length. When completed it gives the effect of tiny daisies strung on a green stem. A charming necklace or collar may be made by stringing the daisies close together and making three or more strands, the lower ones growing gradually longer to give a festoon effect.

Golden-brown Silk and Bead Chain

Materials 1 spool golden-brown purse-silk, letter EE,
Required 1 bunch deep-amber crystal beads No. o,
A No. 8 needle.

Twelve pieces of golden-brown purse-silk two yards long are cut off and tied together at one end. The knot is pinned securely to a heavy cushion or to the back of a stuffed chair. On a piece of silk about a yard and a half long two or three hundred No. o crystal beads of deep amber are threaded, and each end of the silk is tied around a bead to keep the others from slipping off. The middle of the strand is laid under the twelve lengths previously cut, close to the knot, with half of the beads on each side. If the centre strands are fastened to the worker's belt or to a ribbon tied around her waist they can be drawn taut, which will make the knotting easier. Slip one bead from each side up close to the centre strands and tie a Solomon's knot as follows: The end on the left is brought over the centre strands to the right, leaving a large loop before it crosses. The end on the right comes down over the end of the left strand back of the centre strands and up through the loop on the left formed by the left strand in starting (see Fig. 2). The two ends are then held one in each hand and pulled up tightly and evenly. Another bead on each strand is slipped up close to the centre and

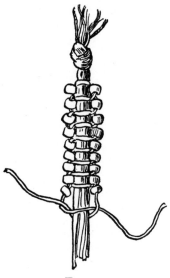

FIG. 2

the same knot is tied. The whole chain is made in this way, pressing the knots as close together as the beads will allow, though not so close as to make the chain stiff. When it becomes necessary to add new lengths to the knotting strands they should

be attached with the weaver's knot (see Chapter
III.).   Touch the ends lightly with glue before
they are cut close.   In finishing the chain the ends
are attached to a clasp or sewed to each side of a
tiny square of chamois skin.

Bead-Weaving on a Loom

BEAD-WEAVING WITH A LOOM

At the left is a belt in green and white. Beside it is a white one with dark-blue diamonds. The chain next to it is white and gold. The smaller one within it has large beads strung at intervals. So has the next chain. To the right is one in pearl-white on amber surrounding an Indian chain in blue and gold. The Indian belt beyond is white with a blue-and-red design. The belt on the right has gold-and-white diamonds on an old-rose background.

CHAPTER III

It is not surprising that bead-weaving on a loom should have become so popular. The process is simple but interesting, the outfit inexpensive, and the results great for the time expended. Chains, belts, and fobs—even card-cases and bags—may be woven, and the work is fascinating. The loom is, of course, to be considered first. There are many on the market, but be careful to choose one that is simple and strong. Perhaps the most satisfactory of all are the home-made looms. More than one weaver has done good work on a loom made of a cigar-box. The sides are cut down to within an inch of the bottom and a small piece of wood, the depth of the box, is fastened inside each corner to support the end pieces. Small notches, an eighth of an inch apart, cut along the top of the ends, hold the warp threads. Six tacks are driven below the notches on the outside of the ends at equal distances apart. Upon these the

27

ends of the warp threads are wound.   A loom that
has proved serviceable may be easily made as
follows by any one with a taste for carpentering.
It has this advantage, one that few looms possess
—it is wide enough to hold the threads for weaving
card-cases or bags.

Bead-Loom

Materials Required

A piece of wood $\frac{3}{8}$ of an inch thick, 12 inches
    long, and $7\frac{1}{4}$ inches wide,
A round stick $\frac{1}{2}$ inch in diameter and 18
    inches long,
2 strips of wood $\frac{1}{8}$ of an inch thick, $\frac{1}{2}$ an inch
    wide, and $7\frac{1}{4}$ inches long,
2 pieces of wood $\frac{1}{8}$ inch thick, $\frac{1}{4}$ inch wide,
    and 3 inches long,
6 smallest picture-hooks,
1 package $2\frac{1}{2}$-oz. round-headed gimp tacks,
8 $\frac{3}{8}$ x 4 screws,
4 $\frac{3}{4}$ x 9 screws,
2 small pointed nails $\frac{5}{8}$ of an inch long,
A thick piece of wire from a package-handle,
2 pieces of florist's wire 12 inches long,
200 black seed beads No. 4–0,
A screw-driver,
Hammer,
Knife and sandpaper.

Choose a piece of white or bass wood three-
eighths of an inch thick, twelve inches long and
seven and one-quarter inches wide for this loom.
Any other wood may be used, but the lighter the

loom the better.   If the wood is rough it should
be sandpapered.   From a round piece of wood one-
half an inch in diameter and eighteen inches long
cut one piece seven and one-quarter inches in
length for a roller and four other pieces two and
three-eighths inches for the posts.   These are
fastened to the base with the three-quarter-by-nine
screws, two at either corner of one end and each

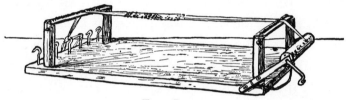

THE LOOM

of the others an inch and one-half from the opposite
end, close to the edge of the sides.   Across these
uprights the two seven-and-one-quarter inch strips
are laid and fastened with four of the three-eighth-
by-four screws.   To prevent splitting, start the holes
for the screws with a gimlet.   Make a small hole at
one-quarter of an inch from one end of each of the
three-inch pieces, fasten the opposite ends of these
strips to either side of the base (at the end where
the posts come exactly at the corners) with three-
eighth-by-four screws, the ends pointing diagonally
upward, striking the posts three-quarters of an inch

from the base.   In the centre of one end of the
roller make a hole one-half an inch deep and around
it six smaller holes three-eighths of an inch deep
and one-sixteenth of an inch from the edge.   In
the centre of the opposite end of the roller drive
a sharp-pointed nail five-eighths of an inch long,
allowing it to project about one-sixteenth of an
inch.   On a straight line drawn lengthwise of the
roller drive round-headed tacks about half an inch
apart, projecting one-sixteenth of an inch beyond
the roller.   A heavy piece of wire, about three and
one-half inches long, taken from a package-handle,
is bent into the shape of a crank.   The end which
is to go into the roller is about three-quarters of an
inch long, the other two angles being equal.   The
end that goes into the roller is sharpened either by
filing or it may be laid on a stone and hammered
flat.   The roller is now ready to be placed in
position.   Pushing the nail which projects from
one end through the hole in the left diagonally
placed strip (as you hold the loom with the end
which has no strips toward you), bring the hole in
the other end of the roller against the hole in the
opposite strip and drive the sharpened end of the
crank through into the roller.   To the right-hand
diagonal strip a short piece of No. 6o linen thread

is tied, and the other end is attached to a five-eighth-inch pointed nail. This is to fit into any one of the small holes in the end of the roller to keep it from turning. One of the gimp tacks is driven into the outer side of each post about one-quarter of an inch from the top and projecting one-sixteenth of an inch. To one of these an end of a twelve-inch piece of florist's wire is firmly attached. One hundred black 4–o beads are strung on it and it is laid along the bar, drawn up taut, and wound firmly around the tack at the opposite side. At the other end of the loom a similar piece of wire, threaded with the same number of beads, is stretched and firmly fastened. These beads hold the warp strands and are better for the purpose in many ways than wooden or metal notches. They hold the threads securely, yet do not cut or injure them; they space the strands better than the

FIG. 3

metal notches, are simple to adjust, inexpensive, and easily obtained.

Let us start with a narrow chain, the one shown in Fig. 3. The beads are 4–o, amber and black.

Four pieces of No. 60 white linen thread well
waxed, a few inches more than the length chosen
for the chain (seventy inches, for example—sixty-
two when finished), are measured off.   In this, as
in all of the woven work, there must be one more
warp thread than the number of beads, so that
there will be a thread on each side of every bead.
The four ends, each tied in a loop, are slipped on to
a tack in the roller, and the long ends are brought
up across the beads on the bar over to the beads
on the opposite bar and down to the hooks, where
they are drawn taut and tied securely.   The loom
is held with the roller end away from the person
weaving, the beads in tiny trays or box-covers
near at hand.   A No. 11 needle threaded with
No. 90 linen thread or Kerr's cotton No. 000
is tied on the left warp thread close to the bar
and brought out to the right, under the other
threads.   Here three amber beads are strung,
brought under the warp threads, and pushed up
between them.   The needle is then run through
the beads from right to left, taking care to have
it go above the warp threads.   The needle is again
brought out to the right below the work, one
amber, one black and an amber bead are threaded
on, pushed up between the warp threads, and the

needle is passed through them from right to left, as before. The same process is continued through the length of the chain, working out the pattern shown in Fig. 3. In joining a new needleful of thread the *weaver's knot* is used. It is made as follows. The joining, of course, is done at an edge of the chain. Hold the old end in a vertical position, laying the new thread back of it, its short end turning toward the left, and projecting an inch or more beyond the v e r t i c a l thread. Bring the long end around in front of the vertical thread, up back of its own short end on the left, and across in front of the v e r t i c a l

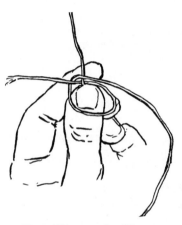

THE WEAVER'S KNOT

thread. All these threads are held in position by the fingers and thumb of the left hand while the right hand brings the thread around. The vertical or old end is now turned down through the loop in front of it and there held by the thumb while with the fingers of either hand the long and short ends of the new thread are pulled up tight. This, if

properly done, will make a knot that will not slip.
To further insure its holding, touch it lightly with
paste or glue.   There are several ways of finishing
chains.   The warp ends may be sewed securely
to either end of a bit of chamois; this is the method
usually chosen by the Indians, or both may be
fastened to one of the small metal clasps used to
hold a fan.   Still another way is to bring the warp

FIG. 4

threads at either end of the chain together, and,
fastening them on the loom in one row, weave a
solid square which will be one bead more than
twice the width of the chain, as one bead must go
between the two outer warp threads thus brought
together.   Beads of the size and colour of the
background of the chain are strung on the ends of
the warp threads for an inch or an inch and one-

FIG. 5

half, making a fringe.   The ends of the warp
threads are then run back through the fringe,

starting at the next bead but one from the last, and finishing off by sewing to the edge of the woven square.

Fig. 6

The design shown in Fig. 4 is for a three-bead chain in 4–o beads. It is particularly attractive if woven in three shades of a colour or two shades and white crystal beads.   Shades of violet, pink or green make beautiful chains.

Another three-bead chain is woven of olive-green crystal beads with a design in palest turquoise-blue opaque beads (see Fig. 5). The five-bead width is perhaps more generally used than any.

Fig. 7

A chain in 4–o opaque turquoise-blue beads has a pattern in opaque white (see Fig. 6).   Another chain in almost the same colouring is woven with the same-sized beads.   It has tiny palm-leaves in black and white on a pale-blue background (see Fig. 7). The 5–o beads make more beautiful

chains. A design for one in white opaque and
a deep shade of blue-green crystal beads is shown
in Fig. 8. On a background of palest blue opaque
beads leaves and berries of mistletoe are charming
(see Fig. 9). The leaves are deep olive-green
crystal beads and the berries the pearly white
beads that look almost like seed pearls. The
same design woven on a ground of gold-lined
crystal and with a scarlet opaque bead instead of
a pearl suggests holly. A dainty chain may be
made from Fig. 10, using chalk-white beads for
the groundwork and dull-red crystal for the design.
Pearly white beads form the background for a
much-conventionalised flower in old-rose with a

Fig. 8

Fig. 9

Fig. 10

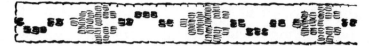

FIG. 11

FIG. 12

FIG. 13

stem of olive-green crystal beads (see Fig. 11).
Blue and white beads are combined in Fig. 12.
The white may be pearly or milk white and the
blue as dull a shade as can be found in a medium-
blue 4–0 bead. A simple design in opaque terra-
cotta looks well on a background of white crystal
beads (see Fig. 13). Pale-amber crystal beads
may be used for the background and opaque or
pearly white and black for the pattern shown in
Fig. 14. A somewhat similar design, but more
flowing, is shown in Fig. 15. It is beautiful
when woven with blue-green crystal and black
beads on a ground of pearly white.

It is difficult to find a good shade of blue.

Dull or dark blue without the disagreeable purple
tinge seems unknown to or unpopular with the

FIG. 14

FIG. 15

Venetian bead-makers. The nearest approach
to a soft blue of medium shade obtainable was
used in weaving the broken diamond shown in
Fig. 16. The beads were crystal and the background also was of crystal, gold-lined. Difficult,

FIG. 16

FIG. 17

perhaps, but rich and beautiful in design and
colour is Fig. 17. The beads are olive-green and

gold-lined crystal. A combination of stringing and weaving makes an attractive variety in these chains. The weaving is begun as usual. Choose a pattern five or seven beads wide—one like Fig. 12 or 16, for example—in which the design is not connected, so that pieces two inches or more may be finished separatley. When one of these sections has been woven the long ends of the

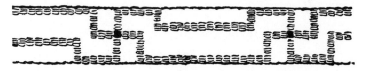

Fig. 18

Fig. 19

warp threads are unwound and strung with beads of a colour used in the weaving. There may be two or three of these strings, the extra warp threads passing through the beads already strung. If the slides are two inches long about five inches may be strung. The effect will be as if the chain were of strung beads with solid slides here and there. The beads should be 4–o, and the warp

strands not coarser than No. 90 linen thread.
Chains seven beads wide are often woven with
beads of 5–0 size. Three designs for these are

FIG. 20

given. The one in Fig. 18 shows the Swastika
in green opaque beads with a single black one in
the centre on a background of white opaque.
Fig. 19 is of old-rose crystal beads with the design
in black. Opalescent beads make the groundwork of Fig. 20, and the simple pattern is woven
in crystal beads, gold-lined. A still wider chain
of 5–0 beads, nine beads wide, is in two shades
of violet outlined with pearly white on an olive-

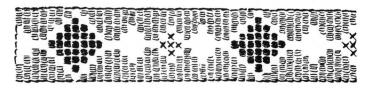

FIG. 21

green crystal foundation (see Fig. 21). This
design makes an attractive one for a belt if woven
three times as wide.

Fobs.—In general the background of a fob should be dark, but one that is charming with

light summer gowns has a white crystal background of 5–o cut beads with an apple and leaves woven on it. The former is of dull-red and gold-lined crystal beads; the

FIG. 22

latter in two shades of olive-green crystal 5–o cut beads (see Fig. 22). The darker shade of green is also used for the tiny leaves at the end of the

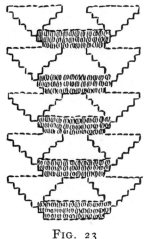

FIG. 23

apple. This design and Fig. 23 (which is in dull-green crystal and chalk-white on a dark-blue background) are repeated the whole length of the fob. Another fob is of dark purple beads for the background and silk warp and woof threads, with a single bee (see Fig. 24) woven near the lower end. The wings and part of the

outline of the thorax are of opalescent beads; the remainder of the outline, the thorax, head, and

dark stripes on the abdomen of black, while the
light stripes are of amber crystal and the eyes
gold-lined crystal beads.

A design of thistles in purple and gray-green

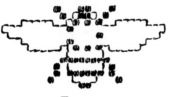

FIG. 24

opaque beads (No. 5-o
cut) is woven on a black
background of the same
beads (see Fig. 25). The
usual method of attach-
ing these woven fobs to
their mountings is to lap the end of the woven
work around the bar and, turning the edge in,
stitch it firmly to the under side of the work with
silk of the colour used in weaving. In making
designs for chains or fobs (where the work is

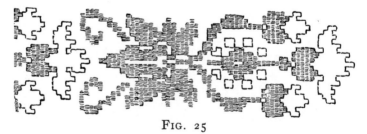

FIG. 25

worn vertically) it must be remembered that
as the beads are oblong rather than round
a design drawn on squares will naturally work
out as if it were elongated.   If the design is drawn

wider than it should look on paper it will work out
correctly. This does not apply so much to designs
that are to be worked in 5–o cut beads, which are
more nearly round.

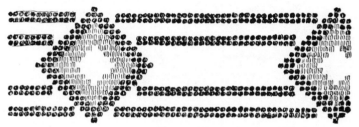

FIG. 26

Belts.—Chalk-white beads make one of the
best backgrounds for woven belts, which look
most attractive with summer gowns. The design
in Fig. 26 may be woven in Indian red, and black

FIG. 27

4–o beads on such a background, or two shades
of green or pink crystal beads on the chalk-white,
will make an effective belt. Figures from an old
rug suggested the design shown in Fig. 27, which

is woven in dark blue and dull red on a white background.   A pretty combination is of chalk-white

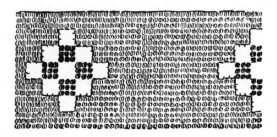

FIG. 28

and gold-lined beads in a diamond pattern on a background of old-rose crystal beads (see Fig. 28). An attractive belt may be made from the pattern

FIG. 29

shown in Fig. 29, using 4–0 dark-blue beads on a chalk-white ground. Green beads on a white crystal background are also effective.

Card-Case

Materials Required	8 spools of pale-blue buttonhole twist, letter D,
	1 spool letter A pale-blue sewing-silk,
	2 bunches palest turquoise-blue beads No. 5–0,
	1 bunch each of black, gold-lined crystal, dark-blue crystal, and dull-red crystal beads No. 5–0,
	No. 12 needles.

The soft colours and interesting design of an old rug suggested this card-case, and fortunately the colours were obtainable in beads. One hundred and one warp threads of pale-blue buttonhole twist, well waxed, are strung on a loom wide enough to hold them. A No. 12 needle is threaded with pale-blue sewing-silk, also well waxed, which is tied to the warp thread at the extreme left. On this 100 turquoise-blue beads are strung and woven into one row. In work as wide as this, where taking out a whole row is quite a labour, two precautions should be used. The beads should be threaded off their original strings with the needle, which will prove whether or not the hole in each is large enough to allow the woof thread to pass through it a second time, when the weaving is done. It will also be wise to use a separate woof thread for each row, tying the two ends together

as the row is completed. A second row of plain
blue is woven, and then the pattern is worked
according to Fig. 30, with black, gold-lined crystal,
blue and dull-red crystal beads, for twenty-seven
rows. This is followed by twenty-six rows of
plain blue, and the case is completed by repeating

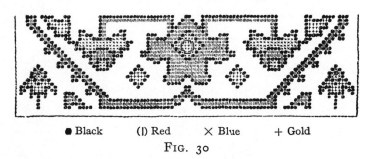

● Black   (I) Red   × Blue   + Gold
Fig. 30

the pattern and weaving two more rows of plain
blue, to correspond with the beginning. The
work is then taken from the loom and a lining
with pockets made of pale-blue silk interlined.
The woven beadwork and lining are then basted
together and sewed over and over at the edges
with pale-blue silk.

Diagonal Weaving Without a Loom

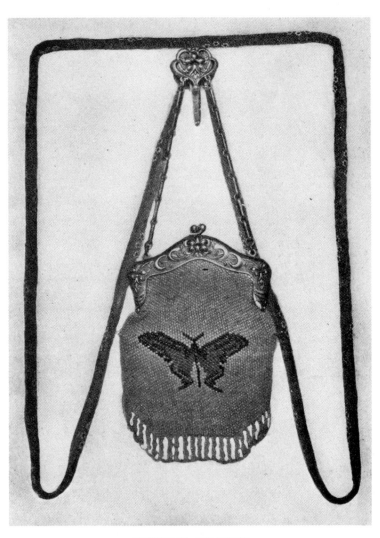

DIAGONAL WEAVING

The side-bag wrought with pearl beads has a butterfly design in amber, black, pale-violet, and old rose. Surrounding it is a chain of violet crystal beads with groups of daisies in white opaque and amber crystal.

CHAPTER IV

DIAGONAL WEAVING WITHOUT A LOOM

A WEAVE like this, that is ages old, must have a fascinating history, if only we could find some one wise enough to tell it. The old Egyptians

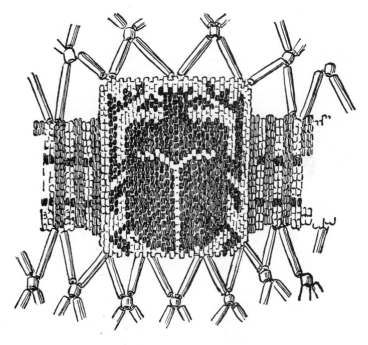

wove with it breast-pieces, which held together the robes of bead network that are found in

mummy-cases.   One may see such a robe at the
Metropolitan Museum of Art.   A scarab in deep-
red and yellow is wrought in this weave on a
background of yellow.   The network is formed
of pale-blue cylindrical beads joined with others
that are yellow and round.   Below the breast-
piece are four solid vertical strips, evidently
intended to represent fishes standing on their
tails.   This curious piece of beadwork came
from the mummy-case of an Egyptian maiden,
the daughter of a priest of Thebes.   We find the
same weave in Indian bead-work, and again in
purses and bags made by our grandmothers.
We ourselves may prove that it is not difficult by
weaving with it chains, fobs, belts, and bags.
The work requires no other material or parapher-
nalia than a spool of letter A sewing-silk, No. 12
needles, a piece of wax, and the beads.   Let us
begin with a chain four beads wide.

Bead   Chain   in   Two   Shades   of   Blue   and   Black

Materials   1 bunch of black beads No. 4–0,
Required   1 bunch of light-blue crystal beads No. 4–0,
            1 bunch medium-blue crystal beads No. 4–0,
            A spool of white sewing-silk, letter A,
            No. 12 needles.

In   all   of   this   weaving   the   width   is   formed

by an even number of beads. The texture is,
like brickwork, laid on its side; the beads do
not follow in straight lines across the width, as in
weaving on a loom, but alternate; if one is up the
next is down. Each bead fits into a little gap
between two in the previous row. In starting
this chain, four light-blue beads are strung, tying
the end of silk through the first bead to keep the
others from slipping off. The work is held between
the forefinger and thumb of the left hand. A
fifth light-blue bead is strung and the needle is
brought through the third bead from right to left.
Another light-blue bead is strung, and the needle
passes through the first bead in the same way
(see Fig. 31). Turning
the work over, another
light-blue bead is strung,
the needle is run through
the next bead but one
to the edge from right to
left, a light-blue bead is

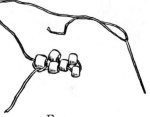

FIG. 31

threaded, and the needle brought through
the bead on the left edge. In the next row
a light-blue bead is strung, the needle passes
through the next bead but one to the edge,
then a black bead is strung, and it runs through

the bead on the edge.   Thus it goes on, the needle
always passing through every other bead after a
new bead has been strung.   In the next row
(after turning the work over as before) string one
light bead, run through the next but one to the
edge, then a black one, and run through the last
bead.   Again turning, the first bead strung
before running the needle through the next but
one to the edge is a light-blue bead.   The next
is a medium-blue bead, and after passing the needle
through the bead on the edge the work is turned,
a light-blue bead is strung, the needle goes through
the next bead but one to the edge, and another
medium-blue bead is strung before bringing the

FIG. 32

needle through the last bead.   The first bead
strung in the next row is light blue, the second
medium.   The succeeding row is made in the
same way.   There are then two in which the
first bead strung is a light-blue one and the second
a black.   Next, four rows in which both the first
and second beads strung are light blue.   There

are then two more rows in which the first bead strung is light blue and the second black. This pattern (see Fig. 32) is repeated the entire length of the chain, using the weaver's knot (see Chapter III.) to attach new needlefuls of silk. The ends may be finished as were those of the

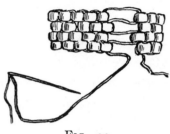

FIG. 33

loom-woven chains, or they may be brought together and the needle and thread run through alternate beads on either end (see Fig. 33). The ends are then drawn close together and the needle and thread pass back and forth through the same beads to where they meet the short end of the silk to which the remaining piece is tied. Another simple four-bead chain is woven of opaque white No. 4–o beads, with

FIG. 34

tiny trefoils of green on alternate sides (see Fig. 34). Fig. 35 shows still another design for a four-bead

chain. It has a background of old-rose crystal
beads No. 4–o, with the design worked in black.
A charming variety of the four-bead chain is
shown in Fig. 36. Groups of pale-blue forget-me-
nots are woven on a background of olive-green.
After weaving an inch of olive-green in 5–o beads
at the beginning of a row, the first bead strung is
pale-blue opaque, the second is an olive-green
bead. The work is turned over, and the first
bead strung is olive-green, the second pale-blue
opaque. After the needle has run through the
last bead in this row the work is turned over and
two beads are strung, the first pale blue and
next to it a gold-lined crystal bead. The next
bead strung is an olive-green one. The work is

FIG. 35

FIG. 36

then turned over, and the first bead strung is olive-
green, the second is pale blue. After passing the

needle through the last bead the work is turned
and two pale-blue beads are strung. The needle

FIG. 37

FIG. 38

now passes through the next bead but one to the
edge, an olive-green bead is strung, and the needle
is brought through the bead on the edge.
Two rows of olive-green beads are woven, and then
another forget-me-not is started in the same way
on the opposite side of the chain. Another two
rows of olive-green are followed by a third forget-
me-not on the same side of the chain as the first
one. An inch of weaving in plain olive-green is
followed by another cluster of forget-me-nots,
and the chain is woven in this way for its entire
length. A six-bead chain is woven in the design
shown in Fig. 37. The figure is blue and green on
an opaque white background of No. 4–o beads.

FIG. 39

FIG. 40

FIG. 41

Another six-bead chain is of white crystal beads
No. 4–o, with a design of forget-me-nots in pale-
blue opaque and gold-lined crystal beads, with
leaves and stems of olive-green and a tiny bud
here and there made of two beads, one pale
violet and the other pink (see Fig. 38). An effective chain is made by weaving a zigzag pattern
(see Fig. 39) in gold on a background of white
crystal beads No. 4–o. The design shown in
Fig. 40 is woven in black and dull-red opaque beads
on a background of dull-red crystal. An attractive
chain may be woven from Fig. 41, using black

beads on a dark-amber background. Another
white crystal chain, six beads wide, has a bunch
of grapes in two shades of purple, with a tiny leaf
of green crystal beads No. 4–o (see Fig. 42). A
dainty six-bead chain may be made from Fig. 43,
using pale-violet crystal beads for the pattern on
a background of pearly white Ceylon beads. Two
shades of a colour, light and medium pink or
violet, woven with the design shown in Fig. 44 will
make an attractive chain. In another six-bead
chain irregular diamonds of dark-blue and bars
of dull red are woven on a background of white

FIG. 42

FIG. 43

FIG. 44

crystal beads (see Fig. 45). A beautiful chain, eight beads wide (see Fig. 46), is woven of pale-

FIG. 45

violet crystal beads No. 5–0. It has daisies in groups of three on alternate sides at intervals of an inch and a half. They are woven of opaque white beads with centres of amber crystal. The upper and lower daisies are made in the same way

FIG. 46

FIG. 47

as the forget-me-nots—*i.e.*, projecting over the edge—while the daisy in the centre comes just to the edge. Designs for two eight-bead chains are shown in Figs. 47 and 48. Fig. 47 is in old-rose crystal beads No. 4–0 on a white crystal background, and in Fig. 48 the design is in green crystal 4–0 beads on an opaque white ground.

FIG. 48

FIG. 49

In making one's own designs to be woven in this stitch it should be remembered that vertical and diagonal lines (as one holds the work in weaving) only are possible; horizontal lines will of necessity be broken and uneven.

The Egyptians in using this weave often strung

two of their flat, disk-like beads at a time instead
of one.   This makes an attractive variation, and
is much quicker than working with single beads.
A design for a belt woven in this way is shown in
Fig. 49.   Either pale-green or white crystal beads
No. 4–0 are used for the foundation; the leaves
are woven in green, and the conventionalised
flower in two soft shades of violet.   Four amber
beads form the centre of the flower.

Side Bag of Ceylon Pearl Beads with Butterfly Design

Materials Required

2 bunches of Ceylon pearl beads No. 4–0,
1 bunch of light-amber crystal beads No. 2–0,
1 skein of dark-amber crystal beads No. 2–0,
1 skein cut-jet beads No. 2–0 size,
1 skein black beads No. 2–0,
1 skein pale-violet crystal beads No. 2–0,
2 old-rose crystal beads No. 2–0,
8 spools letter D white buttonhole twist,
No. 11 needles,
A small tube of paste,
A piece of wax.

The pearl beads of which the greater part of
this bag is woven are known as Ceylon pearls.
They are very beautiful, but not as rare or costly
as the name implies, for they can be bought of
almost any retail dealer in beads and at the same
price as other 4–0 beads.   The bag is woven

round and round, as a stocking or bag is knit, and the widening is done by adding a bead on either side—stringing two rather flat beads together instead of one—and in the next row fitting a bead down between them. In starting, seventy-eight pearl beads are strung on a needleful of white silk well waxed. Another bead is then strung and the needle is run through the next bead but one from the beginning of the string, making a ring. The weaving is continued in the usual way, except that this second row is widened with an additional bead on each side. Two rows are woven plain, then another row widening, one plain row, one widening, one plain, one widening, one plain, and one widening. In this last row two extra beads are added at each side, not, of course, in the same place, but perhaps an eighth of an inch apart. One plain row follows, one widening, one plain, one widening, one plain, one widening, one plain, one widening, one plain, and one widening. A plain row comes next, then another widening, one plain, one widening, one plain, one widening, one plain, and one widening. Ten rows are then woven plain, and in the next row the pattern is begun on the front of the bag, with one dark-amber bead on each side of the centre at five-eighths of an inch from it. The design shown in Fig. 50 is followed. The wings of the butterfly are mostly of light amber, with the lowest beads in the under wings and three near the tip of the upper wings of dark amber. Pale-violet bands run between the two bars of black on the lower wings, ending on the

FIG. 50

inner side with one old-rose bead. Cut-jet beads are used for the body and outline of the wings and dull black for the markings. All of the beads used in working the design are No. 2–o. Nineteen or twenty rows are made after the butterfly is finished, and then the back and front are woven separately, high enough to fit the top chosen for it. It must also be narrowed to fit the bag-top by leaving one bead off in starting each row.   As the metal bag-tops are so different in size and form, the worker will have to use her own judgment in narrowing so as to make the bag and top fit perfectly.   In finishing, the back and front are sewed together at the bottom and the top is sewed at back and front to the metal top.   A double fringe of pearls finishes the bottom of the bag.   It is made as follows:

A needleful of silk is fastened at the extreme left of the bag just below the metal top, and on it fifty of the pearl beads are strung; the needle is then brought through the bottom of the bag half an inch from where it started and out again just back of where it went in.   Fifty more beads are strung and the string is twisted once around the right side of the previous loop.   The needle is then brought through the bottom of the bag half an inch beyond the first loop.   After twisting the strand once around the right side of the second loop a third one is made.   A succession of these loops, each of which is twisted in with the loop to right and left of it, makes a pretty fringe.

Beadwork on Canvas

BEADWORK ON CANVAS
A card-case worked with the finest beads in dull-green and gold.

CHAPTER V

ONE who has a New England mother or grandmother with the characteristic combination of thrift and sentiment which leads her to treasure every bit of old handwork will not lack for examples of beadwork on canvas. There are old bags in bouquet or landscape designs. Sometimes we find one sewed on homespun linen which makes a softer, more pliable texture, not unlike the knitted bags. These are very old. In our mothers' day fire-screens, table-tops, lambrequins, even travelling-bags, were adorned with beads. There was a sad falling off in ingenuity, it seems, from grandmother's time, for we hear that the marvellous roses and scrolls on banners and cushions were "made in Germany," and the backgrounds only left to be filled in.

In the present revival of beadwork wonderful specimens of bead-embroidered canvas have been made. Flowers in bouquet or garland designs are wrought in finest beads of harmonious colours

on iridescent or pearly backgrounds, sometimes
flecked with tiny patterns in gold. It is not
difficult work, but trying to the eyes and also to
one's patience, for it grows slowly. Cross-stich
designs in old fashion-books or in the little French
and German books, which can be bought wherever

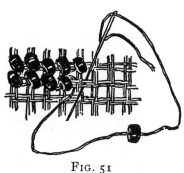

Fig. 51

canvas and beads are
sold, may be used for
this work. Bouquet
designs can be trans-
ferred from old bro-
cade or from drawings
w i t h tracing-paper,
which is marked off in
squares, sixteen to the

inch, and sold by dealers in artists' materials. The
canvas is the finest obtainable and the beads
No. 5–0, preferably those that are cut on one side.
Letter A sewing-silk, well waxed, is used with a
No. 12 needle. If an all-over design is chosen
the design and background are worked together,
but should it be a single bouquet or scroll placed
in the centre or across the piece of work, with
large spaces of background, the design is worked
first and the background filled in afterward.
In starting, the needle is run for a short distance,

say a quarter of an inch, through three or four meshes of the canvas, on the wrong side. A back-stitch is then made and the needle brought

FIG 52

through to the right side. Here a bead is threaded, and the needle, passing down through the horizontal meshes of the next square (see Fig. 51), makes a diagonal stitch which holds the bead securely in

a diagonally opposite position. All of the beads
must slant in the same way, and in order to ac-
complish this the work is turned upside down
in sewing the next row, so that the stitches and
beads will slant as they did in the first one. Or,
if the worker prefers, the needle may be run back
in and out through the meshes from right to left
and start again at the beginning right side up.
A design that is appropriate for a side-bag is
shown in Fig. 52. It is worked on an opalescent
background. The flowers are in three soft shades
of rose-pink, two shades of green are used for the
leaves and buds, a reddish brown for the thorns
and small stems, and green for the large stalk.
A charming card-case is made of dull-green
opaque beads No. 5–o cut, with an all-over design
(see Fig. 53) wrought in gold-lined crystal beads.

FIG. 53

A beautiful and intricate conventional design for
a side-bag is shown in Figs. 54 and 55. It is
worked in two shades of green and black, with a

FIG. 54

touch of gold in the blossoms near the top.   The
background is opalescent.   In the centre is the
wide scroll (see Fig. 54) and at the top and bottom
the narrow band shown in Fig. 55.   The beads

FIG. 55

are No. 5–0 cut.   Those of the lightest green
have a milky texture, almost opaque; the darker
green beads are crystal and the black, of course,
opaque.   The few gold beads used for the blossoms
may be gold or gold-lined crystal.   In the
beautiful old bag from which this design was
taken the beads are as bright and untarnished as
if of pure gold.   Those one buys nowadays are
more apt to become dull, so that crystal beads
gold-lined will perhaps be safer.   A flat garland—
i.e., of one colour without shading (see Fig. 56)—
may be wrought with gold-lined beads on a background of Ceylon pearls No. 5-0.   It makes these
Ceylon pearls look even more pearly to sew them

with pale-yellow silk. In our grandmothers'
day initials were often worked within these gar-

FIG. 56

lands. Charming fringes may be made to finish
these bags. One which will look well with the
bag just described is made as follows:

Fringe With Vandykes.

Materials 1 bunch of Ceylon pearl beads No. 5–0,
Required   1 skein gold-lined crystal beads,
              1 spool of pale-yellow sewing-silk, letter A,
              A No. 12 needle.

If the bottom of the bag which this fringe
is to finish is six inches across, four vandykes,
each made of six diamond-shaped meshes one-
quarter of an inch apart, may be planned. A
needleful of pale-yellow silk, well waxed, is
threaded in a No. 12 needle and fastened at the
left of the bottom of the bag. String three pearl

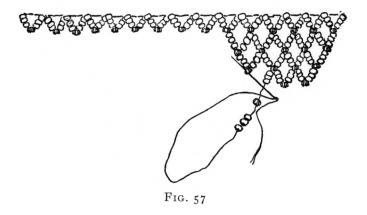

FIG. 57

beads, one gold, and three more pearls, and run
the needle through the bottom of the bag at one-
quarter of an inch from the start. Three more
pearl beads are strung, one gold, and three pearls.
The needle is then run through the bag as before,
one-quarter of an inch from the end of the first
mesh. A row of twenty-four of these meshes is
made across the bottom of the bag. The work is

then turned over, and after running the needle
down through the last three pearls and one gold
bead, string seven beads (three pearl, one gold,
and three pearl) as before. The needle comes
through the gold bead in the next mesh and another
mesh is made. After the fifth mesh has been
strung and the needle has passed through the
sixth gold bead in the first row, it returns through
the last three pearls and the gold bead in the
second row, the work is turned, and a third and
fourth row are made in the same way (see Fig. 57).
The sixth row will bring it to a point. The silk
may here be fastened off by tying it through a
bead, and it may be cut or left to use in making
the fringe. Another needleful is now attached to
the gold bead in the seventh mesh of the first row,
and a second vandyke is made next to the first
one. When four have been finished a double
fringe with twisted loops, like that described in
Chapter IV., will complete the bag.

BEADED BOBBINET

A fascinating material for bags or sash-curtains
may be made by sewing No. o beads on coarse
bobbinet. In sash-curtains it is particularly
lovely, for the light shining through the glass

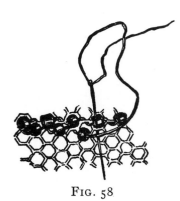

FIG. 58

beads, each of which is set, as it were, in a sexagonal mesh, gives a beautiful effect. Cream-white bobbinet with a design and background of amber beads will be most effective. The stitch is shown in Fig. 58. As the meshes of bobbinet are sexagonal and the texture resembles that of the diagonal weaving in Chapter IV., designs for this work are drawn in the same way. A bee with closed wings (see Fig. 59) will look well on a background of pale amber. The wings are of opalescent No. o beads, the head and legs of cut jet beads of the same size, and the body cut jet and dark amber. There is one dark-amber bead in the centre of the head.

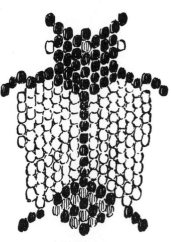

FIG. 59

Primitive Beadwork

INDIAN BEADWORK

The handle of the spoon on the left is wound with strings of beads. Underneath
is a chain of Eastern wampum. The beaded moccasins are separated by a
blanket strip in dark-green and white. At the top is a chain in diagonal
weave, beside it an armlet, and below a broader one. Underneath is a beaded
buckskin bag. At the right a Western wampum chain hangs above a Navajo
silver one. Below is an awl-case, and at the centre a good-luck charm of
beaded buckskin.

CHAPTER VI

PRIMITIVE beadwork is a study in itself, and one of absorbing interest. Does it not make one think to note the resemblance between the flat disk-like beads found in Egyptian mummy-cases and the clam-shell wampum of our own Indians dug up in California and Ohio?

Seeds, beans, and berries were doubtless the first beads used, then shells in their natural state, and later beads of shell and stone ground and drilled by hand. Shell was probably one material of which the old Egyptians made their beads; we know that they made them of stone and pottery. Some, like those used in weaving the scarab shown in Chapter IV., were flat and disk-shaped, others cylindrical. A necklace of these beads which came from the Pyramids may be seen in the plate. Time has given them exquisite, indescribable colours.

More modern, but quite as lovely, is a chain of cylindrical beads, deep red in colour, alternating

with groups of three creamy white shells, which
are so arranged as to resemble the Egyptian
lotus (see plate and Fig. 60).   At the inn of the

FIG. 60

Good Samaritan, on
the road from Jerusa-
lem to Jericho, neck-
laces or rosaries are
sold made of shells
from the Dead Sea
strung with glass beads.   One of these is shown
in the plate.   Another Egyptian chain, modern,
as one can tell by the Venetian
beads with which it is strung, is
from Luxor.   Shells from the Red
Sea of beautiful texture, white and
polished, are combined in an interesting way (see Fig. 61) with opaque
green beads of E size.   The same
beads in green, white, black, blue,
Indian red, and orange are strung in
diamond-shaped meshes to form
bands which alternate with rows of
shells on the costume of a Sudanese
woman which is shown in the plate.

FIG. 61

Larger shells finish the ends of a fringe of beads
at the lower edge, and the whole is lined with a

thick fringe made of strips of leather. It is interesting to notice that the bead-covered handle of the Egyptian fly-brush on the right of the plate is made in the same way (*i.e.*, with successive strings of beads) as the handle of a horn spoon covered by the Sioux. Another point of resemblance between the beadwork of the two continents. To return to our Indian and his beads. He also made, from shell, beads disk-like in form and pierced for stringing—wampum or Indian money. The Eskimo made beads of amber, and the Navajos added to the clam-shell wampum larger pieces of shell in pendant form. Other pendants and ornaments were made of turquoise. Through the Southwest, in Arizona and New Mexico, turquoise ornaments are found rudely carved to represent animals, a turtle perhaps, or a bear. Pinkish shell was highly prized, and sometimes shell pendants were dyed pink. The smaller the wampum the more valuable, because it was more difficult to make. Another estimate of value was its regularity in diameter; the thickness seemed to make no difference. An old writer tells us that in New England the dark-purple or black wampum was made from the small round spot on the inside of the quahog shell.   This was broken away from the rest of the shell, ground to a smooth and even shape, drilled through the centre, and strung.   Three of these black pieces were worth an English penny, six of the white were equal to the same amount, and were current in New England in colonial days. Dentalium shells, which look so like animals' teeth that it is difficult to believe they are any-thing else, are much used by the Indians of the north Pacific coast.   Strings of them are given as wedding presents.   The Thompson and other coast tribes of Indians combine them with glass beads in necklaces and in ornamental work on buckskin.   Carl Purdy says that the "kaia," or Pomo wampum, is made from clam-shells from Bodega Bay.   "It was and still is common cur-rency.   Among not only the Pomo tribes, but their Indian neighbours, many thousands of pieces are coined yearly, and the Indian money-maker is a familiar sight in every rancheria." A link between this beadwork and that in which the Indians use the white man's beads are the silver beads made by the Navajos.   Were they taught by the Franciscan Fathers how to work in silver?   Perhaps, for the monks found silver and made crucifixes of it.   However that may be,

the Navajos are good silversmiths. One of their
necklaces may be seen in the plate. Each of the
large silver beads is made of two coins, usually
Mexican, which are beaten into hemispheres and
welded together. Holes are punched to allow
the buckskin string to pass through them. Flower-
like ornaments form the small pendants (see
Fig. 62), and a large
crescent-shaped pen-
dant completes the
necklace. It is in-
teresting to know that
for generations the
horseshoe has been
an emblem of good
luck to these Indians, and their pendants are
often made in that form.

Fig. 62

Different tribes use beads in various ways.
The Sioux are perhaps the principal bead-workers.
They and some of the other tribes—the Winnebagos and Apaches, for example—do woven beadwork, using a bow for a loom; several warp-strands
taking the place of the bow-string. The beaded
armlets shown in the plate were woven by a
Sioux. On a background of opaque white beads
designs in black, red, green, pink, blue, and gold-

lined beads are woven, and a buckskin fringe is knotted in with the ends of the warp-threads. Another armlet, or bracelet, woven by an Apache (see plate), has a groundwork of opaque white beads, with oblong designs in black, yellow, pink, and green.

A watch-chain made by an Apache is remarkable, not on account of its beauty, but because it is wrought with the same diagonal weave that the old Egyptians used—the weave described in Chapter IV. A good-luck omen in the form of a little green-and-white lizard (see plate) was made of 4–o beads sewed on buckskin by a Sioux. Large glass beads form the feet, which are finished with green feathers. The beaded handle of the horn spoon, already referred to as resembling the handle of an Egyptian fly-brush, was first covered with buckskin and then wound with strings of beads. At the end of each circuit a stitch through the buckskin held the beads in place (see plate). These spoons, made of the horns of Rocky Mountain sheep, were used in Indian housekeeping for dipping grease or serving food. Moccasins of beaded buckskin made by a Sioux are shown in the plate. Dark-blue and white opaque beads are strung and sewed upon them with sinews in a beautiful de-

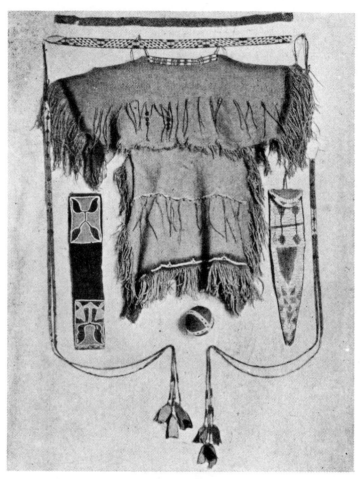

INDIAN BEADWORK

At the top of the plate is a hat-band in open-meshed weave. Below it and surrounding the shirt is part of a Winnebago head-dress. The remaining piece— a band of cloth wrought with beads—is on the left. The shirt is of buckskin, bead-embroidered. Below it is a beaded ball, and on the right a knife-case.

sign. The Sioux use geometrical patterns almost exclusively, while the Winnebagos and Nez Percés are noted for designs of flowers and animals. A beaded strip made by a Sioux to ornament a blanket is of deep blue-green and white beads sewed on buckskin (see plate). An awl-case which a worker in buckskin carried is shown. It is covered with a decoration in milk-white and blue beads. The knife-case (see plate) was also decorated, as was the buckskin bag, with its effective design. The little shirt of fringed and bead-embroidered buckskin is of Sioux workmanship. So are the leggings and the beaded ball, made for an ornament or to be the plaything of a papoose. In the same plate is a hat-band of yellow and blue beads in a diamond-meshed weave, which was probably made by an Apache. An interesting piece of beadwork is the cloth head-piece embroidered with beads and the curiously woven chain in different widths made by a Winnebago Indian for a ceremonial head-dress. Ribbon tassels finish the ends of the chain, which bound the head-piece in place and then fell straight from it in front.

Moccasins for a papoose were often beaded all over—soles and all. It is said that marriage moccasins for men and women were covered with beadwork in the same way.

It will be seen from the foregoing examples how general the use of beads has been among the Indians, whose work is nearer to us and more easily studied than that of any other primitive people. Not alone for personal adornment or for rare ceremonial usage was it done. As in their basketry fine and beautiful work was made for articles of every-day use, so in beadwork we find handles of spoons, knife-cases, saddle-bags, and bridles, beautiful in design and workmanship, witnesses to the art and craft of the Indian.

Candle-Shades

CANDLE SHADES

The shade on the left is made with opalescent and green crystal beads. Beside it is one in which two shades of rose-pink beads are strung on wire to form four medallions. The shade on the right is of pale-yellow raffia with crystal beads of pale-yellow and amber.

CHAPTER VII

CANDLE-SHADES

EVEN those who do not care for beadwork as personal adornment will find that it has a distinct value as a material in interior decoration.

Studying primitive beadwork, we get suggestions for charming candle-shades, decorations for hangings, bead fringes for lamp-shades, and other attractive things. Beads are used effectively in connection with basketry, pottery, and leather work—in fact, the possibilities of this branch of beadwork are only limited by the ingenuity and skill of the worker.

Candle-Shade of Rose-Pink Beads on Wire.

Materials	1 bunch pale-pink crystal beads No. o,
Required	1 bunch deep-pink crystal beads No. o,
	5 or 6 yards of fine florists' wire,
	1 spool No. 90 white linen thread,
	A No. 11 needle,
	¼ of a yard of pink Japanese grass-cloth.

An attractive candle-shade is made of four medallions of wire strung with two shades of rose-coloured beads and finished with a bead fringe. Fine wire is used, such as one can buy by the pound or half-pound of a dealer in florists' supplies. It should be sufficiently slender to slip easily through the beads, for it sometimes passes as many as three times through the same bead. The medallions are made as follows:

On a piece of wire a yard and a quarter long string two dark beads, one light, two dark, one light, two dark, one light, two dark, and one light bead. Fasten these into a tiny ring by winding the short end of the wire two or three times around

the long end close to the last bead. In the second row of the medallion (see Fig. 63) there are t h i r t e e n beads in each loop— first six dark, then a light bead, and another six dark beads. The wire passes through the next light bead to

FIG. 63

the left in the previous row in making each loop. When the circuit has been made the end of the wire passes up through the first six dark beads and one light one in the first loop, and seven dark beads, one light, and seven more dark beads are strung. The wire then passes through the first light bead on the left in the previous row, and the whole row is made in the same way. Care should be taken not to twist the wire. At the end of this row the wire passes up through the seven dark beads and one light one at the beginning of the row. The fourth row is like the third. Eight light beads, one dark, and eight light beads are now strung, and the wire is brought through the first light bead in the previous row. A row of these loops is strung, each having two groups of eight light beads separated by one dark one. The wire now runs up through the first light group, and one dark bead in the first loop and nineteen light beads are strung. It is then brought through the next dark bead on the left in the previous row, and nineteen more beads are threaded. A succession of these loops completes the medallion. The end remaining after the medallion is made is used to join it to the next one. When all four are finished they are bound together near the tops in a hollow square.

Fringe. A No. 11 needle threaded with No. 90

white linen thread is run through a bead in the
lower edge wherever one chooses to begin and
the end tied securely. Twenty light-pink beads
are strung, and the needle, starting at the next
bead but one to the end, runs back through the
beads to the edge of the shade. It then passes
through the next three beads on the edge, and
another strand of the fringe is made in the same
way. A row of these strands, each twenty beads
long and three beads apart, completes the fringe.

The lining is made of pale pink Japanese grass-
cloth. Cut four pieces the exact size and shape
of the bead medallions and lay one inside of each
medallion, catching it with tiny stitches around
the wire between the beads.

Beaded Raffia Candle-Shade.

Materials Required
½ bunch of dark-amber crystal beads letter E,
½ bunch of pale-yellow crystal beads letter E,
About 28 strands of pale-yellow raffia,
A fine darning-needle,
¼ of a yard of pale-yellow Japanese grass-
cloth.

This shade is charming either in pale-yellow
raffia with dark amber and pale-yellow beads or
in pink with opalescent and black beads. The
upper and lower rings are woven with the diagonal
stitch described in Chapter IV., using split raffia

to sew with instead of silk. A fine darning-needle, one that will go easily through an E bead, is chosen, and the bands of weaving are made with dark amber beads for the background and the

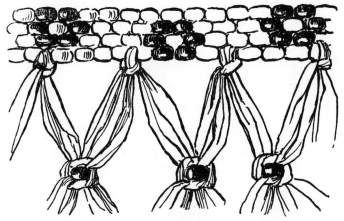

FIG. 64

design shown in Fig. 64 in pale-yellow. When the upper band is seven and five-eighths inches the ends are joined, as shown in Fig. 33, to form a ring. The lower band is joined in the same way when sixteen and a half inches have been woven. Twelve lengths of pale-yellow raffia are cut in halves and each is split lengthwise into two fine strands. Two of these strands are brought through the small woven ring between the first and second bead from the edge and a

single Solomon's knot is made with the four ends
(see Fig. 2). Another pair of strands is brought
through at five-eighths of an inch from the first
one, and this is repeated until the circuit of the
ring has been made and twelve pairs have been
knotted in. The two strands on the right of one
group are then brought beside the two on the
left of the next, and on the inner pair of these
strands a dark amber bead is slipped. A Solomon's knot is made with the two outer strands
at half an inch from the previous row and above
the bead, and another is made just below it. This
holds the bead in a kind of setting of raffia which
allows the light to shine through it. Beads are
strung on the other strands in the same way, and a
knot above and below each bead holds it in place.
This makes a row of half-diamond meshes. Another row is made in the same way, the knots being
each half an inch from those in the row above.
In the next row the beads are strung on the same
pairs of strands as in the previous one, and these
strands are brought straight down together for one
inch, where the strands on either side of them are
tied in two Solomon's knots, one above and the
other below the bead. In the next row the strands
are again separated and the two on the right of

each group are brought beside the two on the left of the next. A bead is strung on each inside pair of strands and held in place by the Solomon's knots, which are half an inch from those in the row above. The strands are now attached to the lower ring as follows: Each of the four ends in a group are brought through the lower ring between the beads and there tied together, two and two, on the inside, so that the edge of the lower ring will not be over a quarter of an inch from the last row of knots. An inch and three-eighths separates the groups. The ends are then cut close and a lining of pale-yellow Japanese grass cloth, the exact size of the shade, completes it.

Candle-Shade of Green and Opalescent Beads.

Materials Required
1 bunch green crystal beads letter E,
2 bunches opalescent beads letter E,
1 spool No. 90 white linen thread,
A No. 11 needle,
¼ of a yard of white Japanese grass-cloth.

The design for this candle-shade was taken from the Sudanese costume shown in Chapter VI. The opalescent and green beads with which it is strung combine beautifully. A strip of bead-work eight and one-eighth inches long and five beads wide is first woven on a loom. The design is tiny green leaves on an opal background (see Fig. 65). When six leaves, each separated from the next by three plain rows, have been woven,

FIG. 65

the warp threads at either end of the strip are tied together to form a ring, and the first row of diamond-shaped meshes is strung. This is made in the same way as the first row in the vandyke heading for a fringe shown in Fig. 57. Seven opalescent beads are used for each loop and the loops are made at intervals of three beads. The next row is also entirely of opalescent beads, seven in each loop. The pattern begins in the third row (see Fig. 66), and the loops are strung with nine beads each. In the fourth row also the loops are made with nine beads, and in the fifth and sixth rows eleven beads are used for each loop. The seventh and eighth rows have thirteen beads in every loop. A fringe thirteen beads deep is then started and strung in single strands two beads apart. This completes the shade except for the lining, which may be of white silk on stiff, transparent paper or white Japanese grass-cloth.

Suggestions for Beadwork on Hangings.

OPEN-MESH BAND OF BEADWORK FOR A BURLAP CURTAIN.

Materials Required
2 bunches burnt-orange opaque beads letter E,
1 bunch white opaque beads letter E,
1 spool No. 60 white linen thread,
A No. 5 needle,
A burlap curtain in the natural color.

This is an attractive piece of beadwork which is simple to make and does not take much time. A network of burnt orange, with a design in white

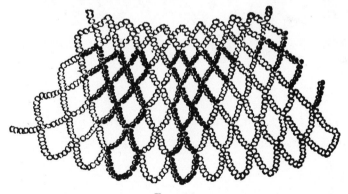

FIG. 66

here and there, is made about fifteen inches from the top of a burlap curtain in the natural colour.

The curtain is first cut straight across at seventeen inches from the finished top, and a hem an inch and a half wide is made. A hem of the same width finishes the top of the lower portion. A needle threaded with No. 60 white linen thread, well waxed, is brought through the lower left

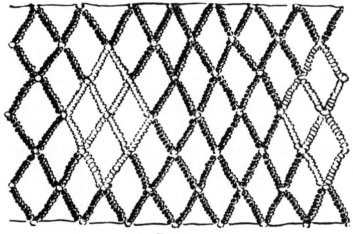

Fig 67

corner of the upper portion of the curtain. One white bead, nine orange, one white, nine orange, and one white bead are strung, and the needle runs through the edge at an inch and a quarter from the start, making one loop. In making the second loop the needle runs through the white bead at the edge, and nine orange beads, one white, nine orange beads, and one white one are

strung. A succession of these loops is made across
the curtain, the work is turned, and another row is
started. In this row the pattern shown in Fig. 67
begins. It is strung in white. The meshes are
made like those in the vandyke heading for a
fringe in Chapter V., except that as the right and

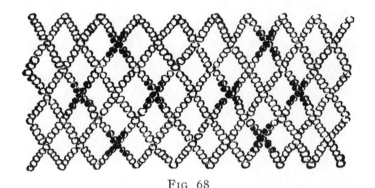

FIG 68

left edges must be straight, at the end of each
row after the first a whole diamond is formed
(see Fig. 67), which makes the beginning of the next
row. At the end of the fifth row the needle, after
making the last diamond, is brought out through
the white bead on the point of the diamond.
Nine orange beads and one white one are strung,
the needle runs through the right-hand top corner
of the lower section of the curtain, up again
through these beads and through the white bead in

the last diamond of the fifth row.   Here nine more
orange beads and one white one are strung, and
the needle is brought through the lower edge at
an inch and a quarter from the start.   In making

FIG. 69

the next and all other upward portions of the
loops the needle runs through the white bead on
the edge, and nine orange beads are strung.   It
is only in the downward half of each loop that one
white bead follows the nine orange ones.   This
method continued across the whole edge binds
the lower section of the curtain securely to the
bead network.   If desired, a narrow strip of
burlap the depth of the insertion may be fastened
to the upper and lower sections at each corner
and the outer edge of the end meshes sewed to
these strips.   Two other designs for such insertions
are shown in Figs. 68 and 69.   The design for a

candle-shade (see Fig. 66) will also be effective, but if it is used for this purpose the meshes must be of uniform size.

Burlap Curtain with Woven Bead Design

Materials Required
4 or 5 boxes of glass kindergarten beads,
A burlap curtain,
A fine darning-needle.

Another decoration for a burlap curtain may be made with the large glass beads that come in round wooden boxes for kindergarten work. Those who have brought from Venice quantities of large glass beads, which are sold there by weight, will find this an admirable way of using them. The simple design in Fig. 70 is given

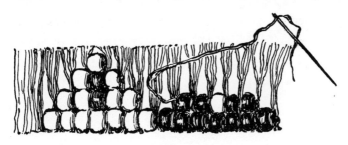

FIG. 70

merely as a suggestion. Others more elaborate and adapted to the hangings for which they are intended will readily be thought of. Choose a soft

piece of burlap, one that has no dressing in it and
is good in colour.   The piece on which this design
was worked was a dark, dull blue.   At the top of a
deep hem draw the threads for an inch and a
half, first cutting them at the selvage.   Thread
a darning-needle with one of the ravelled strands
of the burlap; attach it with one or two stitches
to the lower edge of the drawn portion close to
the selvage on the left side of the curtain.   Bring
it under the vertical threads and out at the right
of the twenty-fourth thread.   String seven white
opaque beads, draw the thread tight, and press
the beads up between the strands as in weaving
on a loom, except that three of these threads,
instead of one, are left between every two beads.
The needle now runs through the beads from
right to left, above the vertical threads, to where
it started.   Here it goes around the three strands
on the left and comes back through the first bead
under the work to the right and out above the
seventh bead.   Five beads—two white, one dark-
green and two white—are strung, the thread is
drawn taut, and the beads pressed up in the
spaces between the warp threads.   The needle
now runs through these beads from right to left,
around the second group of warp threads, back

through the first bead in the row, and under the work. It comes out between the sixth and seventh group of threads above the fifth bead, and three beads are strung, one white, one dark-green, and another white. The beads are pressed up between the warp threads and the needle runs through them from right to left. It then comes around the third group of threads, through the first bead in the row, under the work, and out between the fifth and sixth group of threads. One white bead is next strung, pressed up between the fourth and fifth groups of threads, and the needle is run through it from right to left. Here the thread is fastened off. A continuous row of these figures in four or five different colours may be made across the curtain, the two middle beads in each being the colour of the preceding figures. Isolated designs may also be used.

Knitted and Crocheted Bags and Purses

KNITTED PURSES AND BAGS

The fine old bag at the left has a band of oak leaves at top and bottom and in the middle a design of asters. The two purses on the right are old French specimens with floral designs. Below is a purse of brown silk with conventional design and initials in white beads

CHAPTER VIII

KNITTED AND CROCHETED BAGS AND PURSES

How fortunate is the woman who owns an old-fashioned knitted bead bag! Long forgotten it may have lain in chest or treasure box, but it is now in high favour, mounted in silver or gold. Only the faint fragrance of rose leaves reminds one of its age. Quaint and sometimes beautiful are the designs of these old bags, and the colouring is soft and lovely. Fine silk was used at that time, and the beads were tiny, while the needles were like slender wire. Indeed, my grandmother used broom-wire from a neighbouring factory to knit her bags and purses with, for it was impossible to get needles that were fine enough. One wonders how the women of that generation kept their eyesight, stringing and knitting such fine beads by candle or lamplight. The beads were strung according to the pattern, and direful were the results if one bead was misplaced: the pattern, of course, would be all awry. The texture of these bags, silky and shimmering, is a joy, but not even for the pleasure of giving or owning such a beautiful thing would the woman of to-day spend so much time and pains. There are bags and purses both knitted and crocheted which are most attractive and quite within the range of possibility.

Crocheted Side-Bag of White Silk With Green Beads

Materials Required	1 spool white purse-silk, letter EE,
	2 bunches green crystal beads No. 4–0,
	A fine crochet-needle,
	1 spool white sewing-silk letter A,
	A bead-needle No. 16,
	A metal bag-top.

A dainty side bag to wear with light gowns is crocheted of white silk. The design, a six-pointed star in the centre with a ring of palm leaves surrounding it, is wrought with blue-green crystal beads. It was copied from a very old piece of beadwork, and is made as follows: String one bunch of beads on the white purse-silk, using a No. 16 bead-needle to thread them. Make 2 chains, work 6 sts. around chain. Join on the first single and make a chain stitch before beginning each round. Turn work over. Always work in upper loops of chain. The beads are worked in on the wrong side.

2d round.　Increase to 12 sts., a bead in every other stitch.　This forms points of star.

3d round.　Increase every second stitch, using 2 beads, 1 on either side of point bead, and widen between points always.

Continue same till 7 beads (the width of star) are used, always keeping the s. c. between points.

8th round.*　Decrease star 1 bead, 2 s. c. in next st. 1 s. c., making 3 sts. between star. *

9th round.　5 beads in star, 1. s. c., increase in next 3 stitches, making 7 stitches between stars with a bead in middle stitch.

10th round.　4 beads in star, 3 s. c., 3 beads 1 s. c., 1 widen.

11th round.　3 beads in star, 3 s. c., 5 beads 1 s. c., 1 widen.

12th round.　2 beads in star, 3 s. c., 7 beads 1 s. c., 1 widen.

13th round.　1 bead in star, 3 s. c., 9 beads, 1 s. c. 1 widen.　This finishes star.

14th round.　11 beads, 2 s. c., 1 widen, 2 s. c. The increase is at point of star.

15th round.　1 bead in every stitch.

16th round.　Same as 15th.

17th round. Plain row, no beads, increase every 4th stitch.

18th round. *   3 beads, 1 s. c.*

19th round.   1 bead in every 4th stitch (3 s. c. between).

20th round.   Same as 18th.

21st round.   No beads.   Widen every 4th stitch.

22d round. *   3 beads, 7 s. c. *

23d round. *   5 beads, 5 s. c. *

24th round. *   5 beads, 5 s. c. *

25th round. *   5 beads, 5 s. c. *

26th round. *   1 bead, 2 s. c., 3 beads in middle of five, 4 s. c. *

27th round.   Same as 26th.

28th round. *   5 beads, 5 s. c. *

29th round.   3 beads (in middle of five), 7 s. c.

30th round.   No beads.   Widen every 4th stitch.

31st round. *   3 beads, 1 s. c. *

32d round.   1 bead, 3 s. c.

33d round.   Same as 31st.

34th round.   Same as 32d.

35th round.   Same as 31st.

36th round.   No beads, s. c. all around.

This makes one side of the bag.   The reverse may be crocheted of white silk in the same way but without the beads, or it may be mounted on a white silk bag of the same size and shape.   In either case it is finished with a fringe of green crystal beads, having twisted loops an inch long (see Chapter IV.).

Knitted Bead Purse

Materials Required   1 spool purse-silk, letter EE,
1 bunch beads No. 4–0,
5 knitting-needles No. 22.

The following is an old English rule:

Thread the beads on the silk. Knit 2 stitches on each of 4 needles. Knit 1 round plain. Increase one stitch before and another after the first stitch on each needle. Knit the first stitch, knit a bead on the second and on the fourth all round. A plain round, knitting those stitches at the back that have beads on them. Increase a stitch, knit 2 stitches each with a bead, increase a stitch, and knit on 2 more beads. A plain round. Continue to increase and knit on one bead more until you have 10 on each of the 8 divisions of the star and the plain round is knitted. Increase a stitch, knit a stitch, increase 1, knit 9 stitches with beads, and diminish by turning the next stitch over the last that is knitted with a bead. A plain round. Increase, knit the stitches without beads plain, increase, knit on 8 beads, diminish, increase, knit the plain stitches, increase, knit on

8 beads, diminish. Continue the same, diminishing the beads one in each division, and a plain round alternately till the star is finished with 1 bead at each point; knit 1 round, then turn the purse and knit 2 plain rounds, adding 2 stitches where they will be least observed. Knit 7 stitches, diminish with the next 2 stitches, which leaves 8 on the needle. Leave 1 bead on the silk, knit 7 stitches diminish, leave a bead; continue to do this all round, then diminish before the bead. Leave 3 beads over the 1, diminish, knit 4 stitches, diminish; leave 3 beads, etc. The next round leave 5 beads over the 3, diminishing on each side of the beads to the end of the round; then leave 7 beads, knit the 4 stitches between the beads plain. Next round knit the 4 stitches, add 5 stitches over the beads, knit 4 stitches, and add 5 to the end of the round. Then diminish with the 2 first of the 4 stitches, leave a bead, knit 7 stitches, diminish, leave a bead, and proceed as before.

Crocheted Side-Pocket in Black

Materials   1 spool black crochet-silk, letter EE,
Required   A fine crochet-needle,
               2 bunches black seed beads No. 3-o,
               A piece of black featherbone 5⅜ inches long,

$\frac{1}{2}$ a yard of black gros grain ribbon $\frac{1}{2}$ an
inch wide,
A chatelaine hook.

This is a useful and attractive side-pocket
for handkerchief, keys or eyeglasses. It is simply
made, the bag part being the same width all the
way. At the bottom a single strip of crocheting
about an inch deep makes a background for the
double fringe of twisted loops, while at the top
there is a single width of crocheting in front an
inch deep, and another at the back 2 inches in
depth. The whole bag is made in single crocheting. Begin with a chain of 63 stitches. Crochet

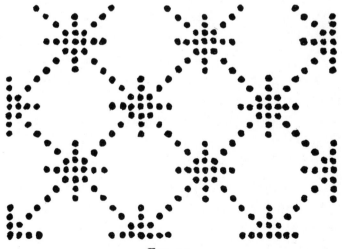

FIG. 71

a straight piece 12 rows deep. Continue the
12th row with a chain of 63 stitches, which is
joined at the other end of the single strip to make
a circle of 126 stitches. Two rows are made and
then the beaded pattern is begun (see Fig. 71).
Fifty-nine rows, continuing the pattern form the
bag. The 60th row has a bead on every stitch,
but it only extends across the front of the bag,
63 stitches. Eleven rows of crocheting without
beads complete the front strip. The back one
is started where the bag part ended and 24 rows of
63 stitches are made, the last row having a bead
in every stitch. The front flap is now hemmed
down inside of the bag, leaving the row of beads
at the edge. Stitch a piece of black featherbone
on the back flap with its upper edge an inch from
the top of the bag portion. Bring the back flap
forward over it and hem the edge on a line with
the top of the bag, sewing it together at the ends.
A row of three stars like those in the pattern may
be worked in beads across the back flap, to correspond with the bag. The bottom of the bag is
then sewed together, and a double row of fringe
with twisted loops covers the single strip of
crocheting. A loop of black gros grain ribbon by
which to suspend it is made as follows. Take

a piece of ribbon half an inch wide and 14½ inches long. Turn in the ends and stitch each firmly to one of the top corners of the back flap. A chatelaine hook fastened at the top of the loop completes it.

Knitted Purse With Star Design

Materials Required	1 spool of purse-silk, letter EE,
	1 bunch seed beads No. 4–0,
	5 knitting-needles No. 22.

The rule for this purse is also an English one. The star which forms the bottom of the purse is made like the first bead purse, then knit 4 rounds plain. Knit 2 stitches, on the 3d knit a bead, knit 3 plain, then a bead stitch, 3 plain, and 1 bead stitch all round. Knit a plain round. Knit 1 stitch plain, 3 bead stitches, 1 plain, 3 bead stitches all round. A plain round. Knit 2 stitches, then 1 bead stitch, 3 plain, 1 bead, the same all round. Then a plain round. The next round begin with a bead stitch; this will bring the stars over the plain stitches. Continue as before.

Crocheted Side-Bag in Gray and Black

Materials Required	1 spool black crochet-silk, letter EE,
	1 spool gray crochet-silk, letter EE,
	1 bunch silver-lined crystal beads No. 4–0,
	A steel crochet needle,
	A silver bag-top.

String half a bunch of silver-lined crystal beads
No. 4–0 on a spool of black crochet silk EE, and

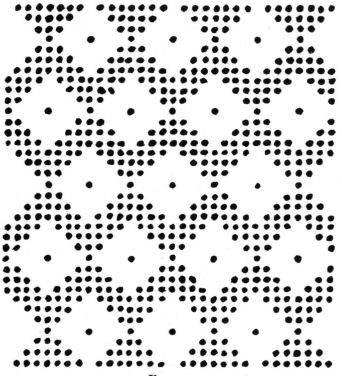

FIG. 72

the other half on a spool of gray crochet silk.
Make a chain of 46 stitches with black crochet
silk. Crochet across this in s. c. in the top loops.
Turn it over and crochet 46 more stitches in the
bottom loops, which will make a ring of 92 stitches.

On the next row begin the pattern, see Fig. 72, widening one stitch at each side. The pattern is worked only on the front of the bag. Six more rows are made and then the black silk is cut and the gray joined for the next stripe. Seven rows are crocheted, continuing the design. A stripe of black follows, the design still continued. The bag is formed of ten of these stripes, five of each colour, every stripe being 7 rows deep. Narrow the bag to fit the metal top selected, and finish the bottom with a fringe of double loops, seven-eighths of an inch deep, each loop twisted in with the one to right and left of it (see Chapter IV.).

Large Black Crocheted Side-Bag

Materials Required

2 spools black crochet-silk, letter EE,
2 bunches black beads No. 2–0,
A steel crochet-needle,
A silver top.

This bag is larger than those already described, but the straight sides make it very simple to

Fig. 73

crochet. String one bunch of black 2–o beads
on a spool of black crochet silk. A chain of 76
stitches is first made, a row is then crocheted in
the top loops of this chain, which is continued
around in the lower loops, forming a ring of 152
stitches. The next row has a bead in each stitch.

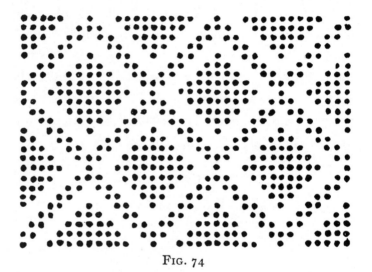

FIG. 74

There are then 5 rows without beads and the
Greek pattern (see Fig. 73) follows for 7 rows.
Five more rows are crocheted without beads and
then the pattern shown in Fig. 74 is made. Five
plain rows are followed by another band of the
Greek pattern. Next 5 rows of plain crocheting
are made and the front and back are crocheted

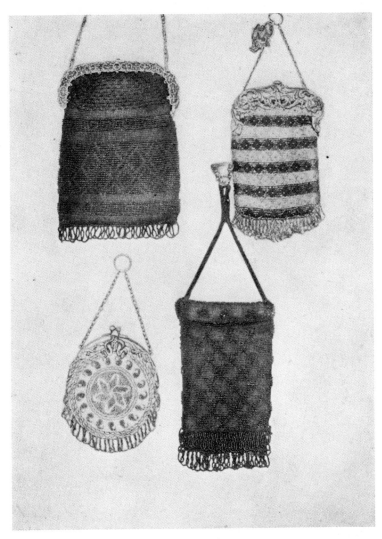

CROCHETED BAGS

At the upper left corner of the plate is a large side-bag of black with black beads. The gray-and-black-striped bag beside it has an all-over design in silver-lined crystal beads. Below this is a side-pocket all of black. The white silk bag on the left has a design and fringe of blue-green crystal beads.

separately and narrowed to fit the bag-top. In
the first row of these separate pieces, 3 stitches
of plain single crochet alternate with two bead
stitches. The next is a plain row. In the third
row the 2 bead stitches are above the plain ones
in the first row, the 3 plain ones being above the
bead stitches. This is repeated, narrowing as
required until the bag
top is high enough to fit
the metal mounting. A
fringe of twisted loops
completes the bag.

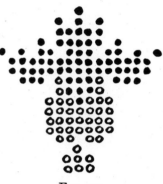

Fig. 75

A simple method of
making a bag in which
the background is of
beads of one colour and
the design in another is
an improvement on the
old way of stringing the beads according to rule.
Suppose the design is to be single thistles (see
Fig. 75) on a background of opalescent beads.
The beads for the background are strung on white
purse-silk. The stitches which form the design
are left without beads, and after the bag is
crocheted the design is worked as if on canvas,
with purple and green beads.

Beadwork for Children

CHAPTER IX

BEADWORK FOR CHILDREN

WOOD and wayside, garden and shore all have treasures in the shape of natural beads for children whom Mother Nature has taught. Their bright eyes quickly find seeds, beans, nuts, berries, and shells to string. Threaded on long grasses or on raffia, these natural necklaces have a charm all their own. It is a pleasant way for a child to learn arithmetic—counting and spacing the seeds or berries.

One family of children, rich in nothing but ingenuity and imagination, used to make beads of the grape-like bladders of an Atlantic Coast seaweed. These were cut close to the bulb, yet far enough to leave a little of the stem on either side of the oval bead, which was pierced while still wet. After the beads had dried for a day or two in the house they were ready for use. When the children were fortunate enough to have a few gold or silver seed beads, three or four of these were strung between every two of the seaweed beads, making a beautiful chain; otherwise the seaweed was strung alone. Melon, apple, and flax seeds, beans and peas, while still fresh, and nuts when green, may be strung, and it is interesting to see what combinations of colour and grouping will result. The city child counts among his treasures wooden boxes of kindergarten beads. These make gorgeous and barbaric chains to wear when he plays Indian. To own a genuine Indian costume may be far beyond his wildest dreams, but he can make one himself, which will be better in some ways. He will have the fun of doing it, and the pride and pleasure of knowing that he can do some of the things an Indian can.

Suppose we begin with the belt. It is woven on a loom—such an one as any boy or girl can make for a few cents.

Bead Loom

Materials Required
An oblong cigar-box, about $2\frac{1}{2}$ inches deep,
4 small sticks of wood, $2\frac{1}{2}$ inches long and $\frac{1}{2}$ an inch square,
16 half-inch screws,
6 small screw-eyes,
6 round-headed tacks,
A sharp knife,
A screw-driver,
Sand-paper.

Choose a good, strong cigar-box, one that is rather shallow, and remove the cover. Rule a line one inch from the bottom of the box on each long side and draw a sharp knife across the line several times, until the upper part separates easily from the lower without injuring the latter. The tops of the sides should then be smoothed

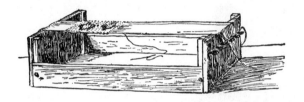

with sandpaper. Fasten each of the small sticks of wood inside a corner of the box to strengthen it. This is the way to do it: Drive one of the half-inch screws up from the bottom into the end of the stick, another into it through the side, and two (one near the top and one lower down) through the end of the box into the stick. On the outside of the box at one end six round-headed tacks are driven in a row, an inch and a half from the top and about three-quarters of an inch apart. In the same position on the opposite end six screw-eyes are driven. Next a row of notches is cut on the

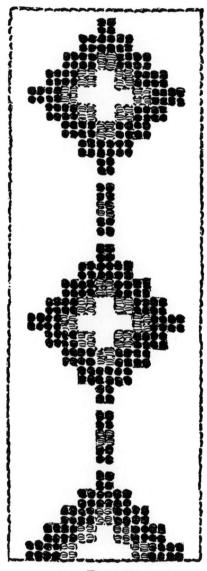

FIG. 76

top of each end of
the loom, about
one-sixteenth o f
an inch apart and
deep enough to
hold a thread. The
loom is now ready
f o r use.   Direc-
tions for weaving
will be found in
Chapter III.   The
b e a d - w e a v i n g
Indians, such as
t h e Winnebagos
and   Sioux,   use
chalk-white beads
for   the   ground-
work of many of
their   chains   and
b e l t s . Suppose,
then,   we   plan   a
white belt with an
Indian r e d a n d
blue   design   (see
Fig. 76) in 3–o
beads.   Belts are

sometimes woven with a solid color. One of chalk-white is particularly good. The shirt, leggings, and moccasins should be all of buck-skin—but we will substitute chamois-skin, which is easily obtained and not expensive.

Indian Shirt

Materials   1 large chamois-skin,
Required   2 smaller chamois-skins,
                1 spool white linen thread, No. 90,
                A No. 11 needle,
                $\frac{1}{2}$ bunch dark-blue beads No. 4–0,
                $\frac{1}{2}$ bunch Indian-red beads No. 4–0,
                $\frac{1}{2}$ bunch white opaque beads No. 4–0,
                28 large Indian-red opaque beads.

In planning this shirt and the leggings and moccasins that go with it, the kind offices of a mother or big sister will be necessary, but once started the work is simple and fascinating for a boy or girl to do. The shirt is intended for a boy of seven or eight, but the pattern can be easily enlarged to fit a boy of twelve or fourteen.

It is made by the pattern shown in Fig. 77, which is drawn on the scale of one inch to a foot. Three skins of chamois are needed—a large one and two of medium size. The large skin is doubled lengthwise to cut the upper portion of the shirt, which should be ten inches deep and a yard wide.

At the centre a slit is cut nine inches long for the neck. The ends form the sleeves. The two smaller skins are next laid together and the lower

FIG. 77

portion of the shirt is cut, the back and front being alike—nineteen inches wide at the top, twenty-two inches at the bottom, and fifteen inches deep. A pencil mark is made at the middle of each lower edge of the upper portion and also at the middle of the top of each of the lower portions. Turn up an inch at each lower edge of the upper portion of the shirt and baste the doubled edge of one side against the top of one of the lower portions, keeping the pencil marks at the middle of each on a line. Now sew these edges together, with No. 90 white linen thread, over and over. The other side is joined in the same way. These over-lapping edges of the upper part of the shirt are kept on the right side. The sides of the shirt are next sewed together with a row of back-stitching

four inches from the edge, and then the edges are cut into a fringe four and a half inches deep at the ends of the sleeves and three inches on the sides and

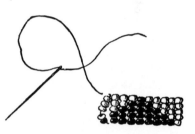

Fig. 78

around the bottom of the shirt. The edge of the upper portion which hangs down over the lower is also cut in a short fringe. Two narrow bands of bead embroidery finish the neck, and there is a band half-way down the lower part of the shirt and one just above the fringe at the lower edge. These are made as follows:

Thread a No. 11 needle with No. 90 white linen thread, make a knot, and bring the needle through to the outside of the shirt, at the right of the neck.

Thread four beads, press them together, and bring
the needle through to the inside of the shirt,

FIG. 79

making a stitch which runs up and down at right
angles with the neck opening.   The needle comes
out again on a line with the place where it went

FIG. 80

in and close to it, four more beads are strung, and
it goes up and in again just at the left of the
starting point, as shown in Fig. 78.   With this

FIG. 81

stitch all the embroidery on shirt, leggings, and
moccasins may be made, stringing different colours
according to the pattern you wish to work.

Several simple designs are given (see Figs. 79, 80, 81 and 82).

In making large patterns, a row of beadwork is wrought like the narrow bands, then below and close to it another row, which continues the design. Another and another row is made until the pattern is completed. This is necessary, for long strings of beads would not wear well and

FIG. 82

would soon get out of place and spoil the design. Narrow strips of chamois are next brought through the shirt in a row (see Fig. 77) an inch and a half apart and tied. A large bead may be strung on the end of each strand, and a knot tied near the tip keeps it from falling off.

Indian Leggings

Materials Required
2 small chamois-skins,
½ bunch dark-blue beads No. 4–0,
½ bunch Indian-red beads No. 4–0,
½ bunch white opaque beads No. 4–0,
A spool No. 90 white linen thread,
A No. 11 needle.

The leggings are very simple to make.   From
two small chamois-skins cut two pieces in the

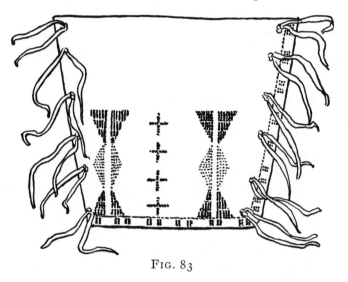

FIG. 83

shape shown in Fig. 83; eight and three-quarters
inches at the lower edge, twelve inches at the top

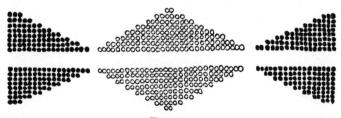

FIG. 84

and twelve high.   They are embroidered with the
designs shown in Figs. 84 and 85, and narrow

bands like Fig. 86 may be worked around the
edge. At an inch from the side edge of the

FIG. 85

leggings, and an inch and a half apart, single
strands of chamois, about eight inches long, are
brought through and tied. Another row is

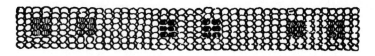

FIG. 86

knotted in along the other edge in the same way.
With these strands the leggings, when they are
finished, are tied on to the young Indian.

Indian Moccasins

**Materials
Required**

1 medium-sized chamois-skin,
½ bunch dark-blue beads No. 4–o,
½ bunch Indian-red beads No. 4–o,
½ bunch white opaque beads No. 4–o,
1 spool No. 25 white linen thread,
A No. 3 needle,
1 spool No. 90 white linen thread,
A No. 11 needle,
A piece of wax.

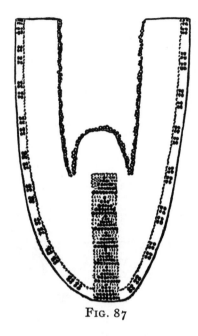

FIG. 87

The child who is to wear these moccasins should stand on a sheet of brown paper and draw around his bare foot to get its exact size and natural shape. This pattern is cut out and taken to a shoemaker, who will cut from it a pair of leather soles. The uppers of the moccasins are then cut from a paper pattern made in the shape shown in Fig. 87. It will not be difficult to make them to fit the soles. These uppers are wrought with some simple design in the stitch already described. The design on the cover of this book is a good one, or the one in Fig. 88. Along the edge the same stitch, slightly changed, makes a pretty finish. A needle threaded with No. 90 white linen thread is brought through the top of the moccasin just below

FIG. 88

the edge. A stitch or two fastens the end firmly. Four beads of a colour used in the pattern are strung, and the needle comes through the edge, from the inside of the moccasin out, a little over a quarter of an inch from where it started, making what is really a long over-and-over stitch. This is continued all around the top of the moccasin, which is then sewed together at the back. The uppers are stitched on the soles with a No. 3 needle threaded with No. 25 white linen thread, well waxed.

Chamois Bag

Materials Required
2 small pieces of chamois-skin,
½ bunch opaque white beads No. 4–0,
½ bunch dark-green crystal beads No. 4–0,
2 large opaque white kindergarten beads,
1 spool No. 90 white linen thread,
A No. 11 needle.

Many dainty little gifts may be fashioned by a girl or boy from small pieces of chamois; bits left over after making an Indian costume.

Heart-shaped pen-wipers, finished around the edge with the stitch with which the top of the moccasins was worked, needle-books made in the same way, and bags. One that may be used for buttons if it is for mother, or for tobacco if

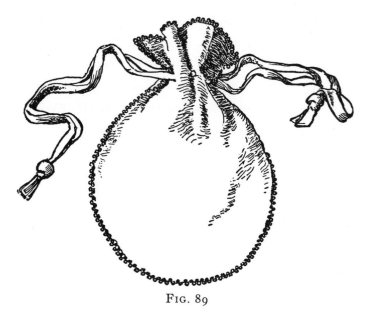

FIG. 89

father or brother Tom is to be the recipient, is cut from two pieces of chamois in the shape shown in

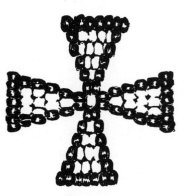

FIG. 90

Fig. 89. A simple design (see Fig. 90) may be worked on the front, or an initial, in green and white beads, or it may be left plain. The back and front should be fitted together exactly and

basted securely. Starting close to the edge at
the upper left-hand corner, the needle is brought
through the bag, three green beads are strung, and
an over-and-over stitch is made. The needle now
comes up through the bead on the edge, two more

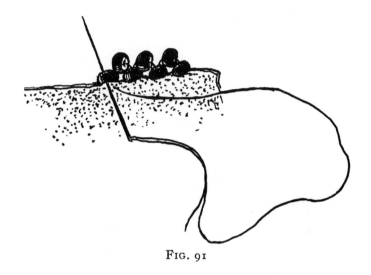

Fig. 91

beads are strung, and another stitch is made
through the two edges of the bag (see Fig. 91).
The whole bag is stitched together in this way and
then a row of the beading is carried around the
edges of the top flaps. Holes half an inch apart
are punched at an inch and a half from the top,
where the top flaps begin, and two narrow strips of
chamois run through them serve as drawing-

strings.   A large white kindergarten bead slipped on to the ends of each strip and held by a knot gives the finishing touch.

Five Bead Chains

Such pretty and simple bead chains as a little girl can make for her best friend!   These strung chains are not as costly and do not take as much time as the woven ones.   Fig. 92 is made with two full length strands of pale-green raffia, on

which are strung large green crystal beads.   The strands are tied together at one end and two fine darning-needles are threaded on the other ends.   As will be seen in the picture, both needles pass through a single bead, then one bead is slipped on each strand.   Next both needles pass through one bead, and so on for the whole length of the chain.

The chain shown in Fig. 93 is also of raffia.   Twenty-two dark amber crystal beads, No. o size, are strung on a strand of split raffia in the natural colour.   Two other strands are threaded with the same number of beads.   The tip end of

FIG. 92

each piece is tied around the last bead to keep
them from slipping off.   At the other end all three
strands are tied together.   They are then braided

closely and evenly for
two inches and a half,
when a bead on each
piece is slipped up
close to the work and
braided in (see Fig.
93).   This makes a
little ornament like a
clover-leaf.   Two and
a half inches more are
braided and then a
bead on each strand is
slipped up and an-
other ornament made.

FIG. 93

The chain shown in Fig. 94 is made of E
beads in two colors.   Half a bunch of each will
be needed, as will a spool of No. 60 white linen
thread and two No. 5 needles.   Three yards of
linen thread in a No. 5 needle are strung with
thirty light beads.   These are pushed down to the
middle of the piece of thread.   Three dark beads
are strung, and then the other end of the strand is
threaded with another No. 5 needle.   One dark bead

FIG. 94

is strung, and the needle passes through the middle one of the three dark beads on the other end (see Fig. 94) and another dark bead is strung. Fifteen light beads and three dark are threaded on one strand; on the other, fifteen light beads and one dark one. The needle on the end of this second strand passes through the middle one of the three dark beads on the first. The whole chain is made in this way.

Another chain (see Fig. 95), a little like this one, may be made with one bunch of green crystal E beads in combination with seeds or with 120 medium-sized oval beads. This is strung with two pieces of No. 60 white linen thread, well waxed, in No. 5 needles. At the end of each

FIG. 95

thread an E bead is tied. Four more E beads are then strung on the strand on the right, and the needle of the other thread passes up through the three middle beads of the five on the right strand

(see Fig. 95), and one more E bead is strung. An oval bead is then threaded on each strand and the E beads strung in the same way as before. The chain is continued in this way for its entire length.

A daisy chain (see Fig. 96) is not difficult to make and is very pretty. Half a bunch each of green opaque beads No. 3-0 and milk-white O beads will be needed and a skein of yellow crystal E beads. It is strung with No. 60 white linen thread in a No. 5 needle. Eighteen of the green beads are first threaded, then eight milk-white beads. The needle now runs down through the

Fig. 96

first milk-white bead, a yellow bead is strung, and the needle passes down through the fifth milk-white bead. The thread must be drawn up tightly. Eighteen more green beads are then threaded and a second daisy is made. The whole chain is strung in this way.

A CATALOGUE OF SELECTED DOVER BOOKS
IN ALL FIELDS OF INTEREST

A CATALOGUE OF SELECTED DOVER BOOKS
IN ALL FIELDS OF INTEREST

AMERICA'S OLD MASTERS, James T. Flexner. Four men emerged unexpectedly from provincial 18th century America to leadership in European art: Benjamin West, J. S. Copley, C. R. Peale, Gilbert Stuart. Brilliant coverage of lives and contributions. Revised, 1967 edition. 69 plates. 365pp. of text.
21806-6 Paperbound $3.00

FIRST FLOWERS OF OUR WILDERNESS: AMERICAN PAINTING, THE COLONIAL PERIOD, James T. Flexner. Painters, and regional painting traditions from earliest Colonial times up to the emergence of Copley, West and Peale Sr., Foster, Gustavus Hesselius, Feke, John Smibert and many anonymous painters in the primitive manner. Engaging presentation, with 162 illustrations. xxii + 368pp.
22180-6 Paperbound $3.50

THE LIGHT OF DISTANT SKIES: AMERICAN PAINTING, 1760-1835, James T. Flexner. The great generation of early American painters goes to Europe to learn and to teach: West, Copley, Gilbert Stuart and others. Allston, Trumbull, Morse; also contemporary American painters—primitives, derivatives, academics—who remained in America. 102 illustrations. xiii + 306pp.
22179-2 Paperbound $3.00

A HISTORY OF THE RISE AND PROGRESS OF THE ARTS OF DESIGN IN THE UNITED STATES, William Dunlap. Much the richest mine of information on early American painters, sculptors, architects, engravers, miniaturists, etc. The only source of information for scores of artists, the major primary source for many others. Unabridged reprint of rare original 1834 edition, with new introduction by James T. Flexner, and 394 new illustrations. Edited by Rita Weiss. 6⅝ x 9⅝.
21695-0, 21696-9, 21697-7 Three volumes, Paperbound $13.50

EPOCHS OF CHINESE AND JAPANESE ART, Ernest F. Fenollosa. From primitive Chinese art to the 20th century, thorough history, explanation of every important art period and form, including Japanese woodcuts; main stress on China and Japan, but Tibet, Korea also included. Still unexcelled for its detailed, rich coverage of cultural background, aesthetic elements, diffusion studies, particularly of the historical period. 2nd, 1913 edition. 242 illustrations. lii + 439pp. of text.
20364-6, 20365-4 Two volumes, Paperbound $6.00

THE GENTLE ART OF MAKING ENEMIES, James A. M. Whistler. Greatest wit of his day deflates Oscar Wilde, Ruskin, Swinburne; strikes back at inane critics, exhibitions, art journalism; aesthetics of impressionist revolution in most striking form. Highly readable classic by great painter. Reproduction of edition designed by Whistler. Introduction by Alfred Werner. xxxvi + 334pp.
21875-9 Paperbound $2.50

VISUAL ILLUSIONS: THEIR CAUSES, CHARACTERISTICS, AND APPLICATIONS, Matthew Luckiesh. Thorough description and discussion of optical illusion, geometric and perspective, particularly; size and shape distortions, illusions of color, of motion; natural illusions; use of illusion in art and magic, industry, etc. Most useful today with op art, also for classical art. Scores of effects illustrated. Introduction by William H. Ittleson. 100 illustrations. xxi + 252pp.

21530-X Paperbound $2.00

A HANDBOOK OF ANATOMY FOR ART STUDENTS, Arthur Thomson. Thorough, virtually exhaustive coverage of skeletal structure, musculature, etc. Full text, supplemented by anatomical diagrams and drawings and by photographs of undraped figures. Unique in its comparison of male and female forms, pointing out differences of contour, texture, form. 211 figures, 40 drawings, 86 photographs. xx + 459pp. 5⅜ x 8⅜.

21163-0 Paperbound $3.50

150 MASTERPIECES OF DRAWING, Selected by Anthony Toney. Full page reproductions of drawings from the early 16th to the end of the 18th century, all beautifully reproduced: Rembrandt, Michelangelo, Dürer, Fragonard, Urs, Graf, Wouwerman, many others. First-rate browsing book, model book for artists. xviii + 150pp. 8⅜ x 11¼.

21032-4 Paperbound $2.50

THE LATER WORK OF AUBREY BEARDSLEY, Aubrey Beardsley. Exotic, erotic, ironic masterpieces in full maturity: Comedy Ballet, Venus and Tannhauser, Pierrot, Lysistrata, Rape of the Lock, Savoy material, Ali Baba, Volpone, etc. This material revolutionized the art world, and is still powerful, fresh, brilliant. With *The Early Work,* all Beardsley's finest work. 174 plates, 2 in color. xiv + 176pp. 8⅛ x 11.

21817-1 Paperbound $3.00

DRAWINGS OF REMBRANDT, Rembrandt van Rijn. Complete reproduction of fabulously rare edition by Lippmann and Hofstede de Groot, completely reedited, updated, improved by Prof. Seymour Slive, Fogg Museum. Portraits, Biblical sketches, landscapes, Oriental types, nudes, episodes from classical mythology—All Rembrandt's fertile genius. Also selection of drawings by his pupils and followers. "Stunning volumes," *Saturday Review.* 550 illustrations. lxxviii + 552pp. 9⅛ x 12¼.

21485-0, 21486-9 Two volumes, Paperbound $7.00

THE DISASTERS OF WAR, Francisco Goya. One of the masterpieces of Western civilization—83 etchings that record Goya's shattering, bitter reaction to the Napoleonic war that swept through Spain after the insurrection of 1808 and to war in general. Reprint of the first edition, with three additional plates from Boston's Museum of Fine Arts. All plates facsimile size. Introduction by Philip Hofer, Fogg Museum. v + 97pp. 9⅜ x 8¼.

21872-4 Paperbound $2.00

GRAPHIC WORKS OF ODILON REDON. Largest collection of Redon's graphic works ever assembled: 172 lithographs, 28 etchings and engravings, 9 drawings. These include some of his most famous works. All the plates from *Odilon Redon: oeuvre graphique complet,* plus additional plates. New introduction and caption translations by Alfred Werner. 209 illustrations. xxvii + 209pp. 9⅛ x 12¼.

21966-8 Paperbound $4.00

DESIGN BY ACCIDENT; A BOOK OF "ACCIDENTAL EFFECTS" FOR ARTISTS AND DESIGNERS, James F. O'Brien. Create your own unique, striking, imaginative effects by "controlled accident" interaction of materials: paints and lacquers, oil and water based paints, splatter, crackling materials, shatter, similar items. Everything you do will be different; first book on this limitless art, so useful to both fine artist and commercial artist. Full instructions. 192 plates showing "accidents," 8 in color. viii + 215pp. 8⅜ x 11¼.   21942-9 Paperbound $3.50

THE BOOK OF SIGNS, Rudolf Koch. Famed German type designer draws 493 beautiful symbols: religious, mystical, alchemical, imperial, property marks, runes, etc. Remarkable fusion of traditional and modern. Good for suggestions of timelessness, smartness, modernity. Text. vi + 104pp. 6⅛ x 9¼.
                                                           20162-7 Paperbound $1.25

HISTORY OF INDIAN AND INDONESIAN ART, Ananda K. Coomaraswamy. An unabridged republication of one of the finest books by a great scholar in Eastern art. Rich in descriptive material, history, social backgrounds; Sunga reliefs, Rajput paintings, Gupta temples, Burmese frescoes, textiles, jewelry, sculpture, etc. 400 photos. viii + 423pp. 6⅜ x 9¾.   21436-2 Paperbound $4.00

PRIMITIVE ART, Franz Boas. America's foremost anthropologist surveys textiles, ceramics, woodcarving, basketry, metalwork, etc.; patterns, technology, creation of symbols, style origins. All areas of world, but very full on Northwest Coast Indians. More than 350 illustrations of baskets, boxes, totem poles, weapons, etc. 378 pp.
                                                           20025-6 Paperbound $3.00

THE GENTLEMAN AND CABINET MAKER'S DIRECTOR, Thomas Chippendale. Full reprint (third edition, 1762) of most influential furniture book of all time, by master cabinetmaker. 200 plates, illustrating chairs, sofas, mirrors, tables, cabinets, plus 24 photographs of surviving pieces. Biographical introduction by N. Bienenstock. vi + 249pp. 9⅞ x 12¾.   21601-2 Paperbound $4.00

AMERICAN ANTIQUE FURNITURE, Edgar G. Miller, Jr. The basic coverage of all American furniture before 1840. Individual chapters cover type of furniture—clocks, tables, sideboards, etc.—chronologically, with inexhaustible wealth of data. More than 2100 photographs, all identified, commented on. Essential to all early American collectors. Introduction by H. E. Keyes. vi + 1106pp. 7⅞ x 10¾.
                              21599-7, 21600-4 Two volumes, Paperbound $11.00

PENNSYLVANIA DUTCH AMERICAN FOLK ART, Henry J. Kauffman. 279 photos, 28 drawings of tulipware, Fraktur script, painted tinware, toys, flowered furniture, quilts, samplers, hex signs, house interiors, etc. Full descriptive text. Excellent for tourist, rewarding for designer, collector. Map. 146pp. 7⅞ x 10¾.
                                                           21205-X Paperbound $2.50

EARLY NEW ENGLAND GRAVESTONE RUBBINGS, Edmund V. Gillon, Jr. 43 photographs, 226 carefully reproduced rubbings show heavily symbolic, sometimes macabre early gravestones, up to early 19th century. Remarkable early American primitive art, occasionally strikingly beautiful; always powerful. Text. xxvi + 207pp. 8⅜ x 11¼.   21380-3 Paperbound $3.50

ALPHABETS AND ORNAMENTS, Ernst Lehner. Well-known pictorial source for decorative alphabets, script examples, cartouches, frames, decorative title pages, calligraphic initials, borders, similar material. 14th to 19th century, mostly European. Useful in almost any graphic arts designing, varied styles. 750 illustrations. 256pp. 7 x 10. 21905-4 Paperbound $4.00

PAINTING: A CREATIVE APPROACH, Norman Colquhoun. For the beginner simple guide provides an instructive approach to painting: major stumbling blocks for beginner; overcoming them, technical points; paints and pigments; oil painting; watercolor and other media and color. New section on "plastic" paints. Glossary. Formerly *Paint Your Own Pictures.* 221pp. 22000-1 Paperbound $1.75

THE ENJOYMENT AND USE OF COLOR, Walter Sargent. Explanation of the relations between colors themselves and between colors in nature and art, including hundreds of little-known facts about color values, intensities, effects of high and low illumination, complementary colors. Many practical hints for painters, references to great masters. 7 color plates, 29 illustrations. x + 274pp. 20944-X Paperbound $2.75

THE NOTEBOOKS OF LEONARDO DA VINCI, compiled and edited by Jean Paul Richter. 1566 extracts from original manuscripts reveal the full range of Leonardo's versatile genius: all his writings on painting, sculpture, architecture, anatomy, astronomy, geography, topography, physiology, mining, music, etc., in both Italian and English, with 186 plates of manuscript pages and more than 500 additional drawings. Includes studies for the Last Supper, the lost Sforza monument, and other works. Total of xlvii + 866pp. 7⅞ x 10¾. 22572-0, 22573-9 Two volumes, Paperbound $10.00

MONTGOMERY WARD CATALOGUE OF 1895. Tea gowns, yards of flannel and pillow-case lace, stereoscopes, books of gospel hymns, the New Improved Singer Sewing Machine, side saddles, milk skimmers, straight-edged razors, high-button shoes, spittoons, and on and on . . . listing some 25,000 items, practically all illustrated. Essential to the shoppers of the 1890's, it is our truest record of the spirit of the period. Unaltered reprint of Issue No. 57, Spring and Summer 1895. Introduction by Boris Emmet. Innumerable illustrations. xiii + 624pp. 8½ x 11⅝. 22377-9 Paperbound $6.95

THE CRYSTAL PALACE EXHIBITION ILLUSTRATED CATALOGUE (LONDON, 1851). One of the wonders of the modern world—the Crystal Palace Exhibition in which all the nations of the civilized world exhibited their achievements in the arts and sciences—presented in an equally important illustrated catalogue. More than 1700 items pictured with accompanying text—ceramics, textiles, cast-iron work, carpets, pianos, sleds, razors, wall-papers, billiard tables, beehives, silverware and hundreds of other artifacts—represent the focal point of Victorian culture in the Western World. Probably the largest collection of Victorian decorative art ever assembled— indispensable for antiquarians and designers. Unabridged republication of the Art-Journal Catalogue of the Great Exhibition of 1851, with all terminal essays. New introduction by John Gloag, F.S.A. xxxiv + 426pp. 9 x 12. 22503-8 Paperbound $4.50

A History of Costume, Carl Köhler. Definitive history, based on surviving pieces of clothing primarily, and paintings, statues, etc. secondarily. Highly readable text, supplemented by 594 illustrations of costumes of the ancient Mediterranean peoples, Greece and Rome, the Teutonic prehistoric period; costumes of the Middle Ages, Renaissance, Baroque, 18th and 19th centuries. Clear, measured patterns are provided for many clothing articles. Approach is practical throughout. Enlarged by Emma von Sichart. 464pp. 21030-8 Paperbound $3.50

Oriental Rugs, Antique and Modern, Walter A. Hawley. A complete and authoritative treatise on the Oriental rug—where they are made, by whom and how, designs and symbols, characteristics in detail of the six major groups, how to distinguish them and how to buy them. Detailed technical data is provided on periods, weaves, warps, wefts, textures, sides, ends and knots, although no technical background is required for an understanding. 11 color plates, 80 halftones, 4 maps. vi + 320pp. 6⅛ x 9⅛. 22366-3 Paperbound $5.00

Ten Books on Architecture, Vitruvius. By any standards the most important book on architecture ever written. Early Roman discussion of aesthetics of building, construction methods, orders, sites, and every other aspect of architecture has inspired, instructed architecture for about 2,000 years. Stands behind Palladio, Michelangelo, Bramante, Wren, countless others. Definitive Morris H. Morgan translation. 68 illustrations. xii + 331pp. 20645-9 Paperbound $2.50

The Four Books of Architecture, Andrea Palladio. Translated into every major Western European language in the two centuries following its publication in 1570, this has been one of the most influential books in the history of architecture. Complete reprint of the 1738 Isaac Ware edition. New introduction by Adolf Placzek, Columbia Univ. 216 plates. xxii + 110pp. of text. 9½ x 12¾. 21308-0 Clothbound $10.00

Sticks and Stones: A Study of American Architecture and Civilization, Lewis Mumford.One of the great classics of American cultural history. American architecture from the medieval-inspired earliest forms to the early 20th century; evolution of structure and style, and reciprocal influences on environment. 21 photographic illustrations. 238pp. 20202-X Paperbound $2.00

The American Builder's Companion, Asher Benjamin. The most widely used early 19th century architectural style and source book, for colonial up into Greek Revival periods. Extensive development of geometry of carpentering, construction of sashes, frames, doors, stairs; plans and elevations of domestic and other buildings. Hundreds of thousands of houses were built according to this book, now invaluable to historians, architects, restorers, etc. 1827 edition. 59 plates. 114pp. 7⅞ x 10¾. 22236-5 Paperbound $3.00

Dutch Houses in the Hudson Valley Before 1776, Helen Wilkinson Reynolds. The standard survey of the Dutch colonial house and outbuildings, with constructional features, decoration, and local history associated with individual homesteads. Introduction by Franklin D. Roosevelt. Map. 150 illustrations. 469pp. 6⅝ x 9¼. 21469-9 Paperbound $4.00

THE ARCHITECTURE OF COUNTRY HOUSES, Andrew J. Downing. Together with Vaux's *Villas and Cottages* this is the basic book for Hudson River Gothic architecture of the middle Victorian period. Full, sound discussions of general aspects of housing, architecture, style, decoration, furnishing, together with scores of detailed house plans, illustrations of specific buildings, accompanied by full text. Perhaps the most influential single American architectural book. 1850 edition. Introduction by J. Stewart Johnson. 321 figures, 34 architectural designs. xvi + 560pp.

22003-6 Paperbound $4.00

LOST EXAMPLES OF COLONIAL ARCHITECTURE, John Mead Howells. Full-page photographs of buildings that have disappeared or been so altered as to be denatured, including many designed by major early American architects. 245 plates. xvii + 248pp. 7⅞ x 10¾. 21143-6 Paperbound $3.50

DOMESTIC ARCHITECTURE OF THE AMERICAN COLONIES AND OF THE EARLY REPUBLIC, Fiske Kimball. Foremost architect and restorer of Williamsburg and Monticello covers nearly 200 homes between 1620-1825. Architectural details, construction, style features, special fixtures, floor plans, etc. Generally considered finest work in its area. 219 illustrations of houses, doorways, windows, capital mantels. xx + 314pp. 7⅞ x 10¾. 21743-4 Paperbound $4.00

EARLY AMERICAN ROOMS: 1650-1858, edited by Russell Hawes Kettell. Tour of 12 rooms, each representative of a different era in American history and each furnished, decorated, designed and occupied in the style of the era. 72 plans and elevations, 8-page color section, etc., show fabrics, wall papers, arrangements, etc. Full descriptive text. xvii + 200pp. of text. 8⅜ x 11¼.

21633-0 Paperbound $5.00

THE FITZWILLIAM VIRGINAL BOOK, edited by J. Fuller Maitland and W. B. Squire. Full modern printing of famous early 17th-century ms. volume of 300 works by Morley, Byrd, Bull, Gibbons, etc. For piano or other modern keyboard instrument; easy to read format. xxxvi + 938pp. 8⅜ x 11.

21068-5, 21069-3 Two volumes, Paperbound $10.00

KEYBOARD MUSIC, Johann Sebastian Bach. Bach Gesellschaft edition. A rich selection of Bach's masterpieces for the harpsichord: the six English Suites, six French Suites, the six Partitas (Clavierübung part I), the Goldberg Variations (Clavierübung part IV), the fifteen Two-Part Inventions and the fifteen Three-Part Sinfonias. Clearly reproduced on large sheets with ample margins; eminently playable. vi + 312pp. 8⅛ x 11. 22360-4 Paperbound $5.00

THE MUSIC OF BACH: AN INTRODUCTION, Charles Sanford Terry. A fine, nontechnical introduction to Bach's music, both instrumental and vocal. Covers organ music, chamber music, passion music, other types. Analyzes themes, developments, innovations. x + 114pp. 21075-8 Paperbound $1.25

BEETHOVEN AND HIS NINE SYMPHONIES, Sir George Grove. Noted British musicologist provides best history, analysis, commentary on symphonies. Very thorough, rigorously accurate; necessary to both advanced student and amateur music lover. 436 musical passages. vii + 407 pp. 20334-4 Paperbound $2.75

JOHANN SEBASTIAN BACH, Philipp Spitta. One of the great classics of musicology, this definitive analysis of Bach's music (and life) has never been surpassed. Lucid, nontechnical analyses of hundreds of pieces (30 pages devoted to St. Matthew Passion, 26 to B Minor Mass). Also includes major analysis of 18th-century music. 450 musical examples. 40-page musical supplement. Total of xx + 1799pp.
(EUK) 22278-0, 22279-9 Two volumes, Clothbound $17.50

MOZART AND HIS PIANO CONCERTOS, Cuthbert Girdlestone. The only full-length study of an important area of Mozart's creativity. Provides detailed analyses of all 23 concertos, traces inspirational sources. 417 musical examples. Second edition. 509pp. (USO) 21271-8 Paperbound $3.50

THE PERFECT WAGNERITE: A COMMENTARY ON THE NIBLUNG'S RING, George Bernard Shaw. Brilliant and still relevant criticism in remarkable essays on Wagner's Ring cycle, Shaw's ideas on political and social ideology behind the plots, role of Leitmotifs, vocal requisites, etc. Prefaces. xxi + 136pp.
21707-8 Paperbound $1.50

DON GIOVANNI, W. A. Mozart. Complete libretto, modern English translation; biographies of composer and librettist; accounts of early performances and critical reaction. Lavishly illustrated. All the material you need to understand and appreciate this great work. Dover Opera Guide and Libretto Series; translated and introduced by Ellen Bleiler. 92 illustrations. 209pp.
21134-7 Paperbound $1.50

HIGH FIDELITY SYSTEMS: A LAYMAN'S GUIDE, Roy F. Allison. All the basic information you need for setting up your own audio system: high fidelity and stereo record players, tape records, F.M. Connections, adjusting tone arm, cartridge, checking needle alignment, positioning speakers, phasing speakers, adjusting hums, trouble-shooting, maintenance, and similar topics. Enlarged 1965 edition. More than 50 charts, diagrams, photos. iv + 91pp. 21514-8 Paperbound $1.25

REPRODUCTION OF SOUND, Edgar Villchur. Thorough coverage for laymen of high fidelity systems, reproducing systems in general, needles, amplifiers, preamps, loudspeakers, feedback, explaining physical background. "A rare talent for making technicalities vividly comprehensible," R. Darrell, *High Fidelity*. 69 figures. iv + 92pp. 21515-6 Paperbound $1.25

HEAR ME TALKIN' TO YA: THE STORY OF JAZZ AS TOLD BY THE MEN WHO MADE IT, Nat Shapiro and Nat Hentoff. Louis Armstrong, Fats Waller, Jo Jones, Clarence Williams, Billy Holiday, Duke Ellington, Jelly Roll Morton and dozens of other jazz greats tell how it was in Chicago's South Side, New Orleans, depression Harlem and the modern West Coast as jazz was born and grew. xvi + 429pp.
21726-4 Paperbound $2.50

FABLES OF AESOP, translated by Sir Roger L'Estrange. A reproduction of the very rare 1931 Paris edition; a selection of the most interesting fables, together with 50 imaginative drawings by Alexander Calder. v + 128pp. 6½x9¼.
21780-9 Paperbound $1.50

AGAINST THE GRAIN (A REBOURS), Joris K. Huysmans. Filled with weird images, evidences of a bizarre imagination, exotic experiments with hallucinatory drugs, rich tastes and smells and the diversions of its sybarite hero Duc Jean des Esseintes, this classic novel pushed 19th-century literary decadence to its limits. Full un-abridged edition. Do not confuse this with abridged editions generally sold. Intro-duction by Havelock Ellis. xlix + 206pp. 22190-3 Paperbound $2.00

VARIORUM SHAKESPEARE: HAMLET. Edited by Horace H. Furness; a landmark of American scholarship. Exhaustive footnotes and appendices treat all doubtful words and phrases, as well as suggested critical emendations throughout the play's history. First volume contains editor's own text, collated with all Quartos and Folios. Second volume contains full first Quarto, translations of Shakespeare's sources (Belleforest, and Saxo Grammaticus), Der Bestrafte Brudermord, and many essays on critical and historical points of interest by major authorities of past and present. Includes details of staging and costuming over the years. By far the best edition available for serious students of Shakespeare. Total of xx + 905pp.
21004-9, 21005-7, 2 volumes, Paperbound $7.00

A LIFE OF WILLIAM SHAKESPEARE, Sir Sidney Lee. This is the standard life of Shakespeare, summarizing everything known about Shakespeare and his plays. Incredibly rich in material, broad in coverage, clear and judicious, it has served thousands as the best introduction to Shakespeare. 1931 edition. 9 plates. xxix + 792pp. (USO) 21967-4 Paperbound $3.75

MASTERS OF THE DRAMA, John Gassner. Most comprehensive history of the drama in print, covering every tradition from Greeks to modern Europe and America, including India, Far East, etc. Covers more than 800 dramatists, 2000 plays, with biographical material, plot summaries, theatre history, criticism, etc. "Best of its kind in English," *New Republic*. 77 illustrations. xxii + 890pp.
20100-7 Clothbound $8.50

THE EVOLUTION OF THE ENGLISH LANGUAGE, George McKnight. The growth of English, from the 14th century to the present. Unusual, non-technical account presents basic information in very interesting form: sound shifts, change in grammar and syntax, vocabulary growth, similar topics. Abundantly illustrated with quota-tions. Formerly *Modern English in the Making*. xii + 590pp.
21932-1 Paperbound $3.50

AN ETYMOLOGICAL DICTIONARY OF MODERN ENGLISH, Ernest Weekley. Fullest, richest work of its sort, by foremost British lexicographer. Detailed word histories, including many colloquial and archaic words; extensive quotations. Do not con-fuse this with the Concise Etymological Dictionary, which is much abridged. Total of xxvii + 830pp. 6½ x 9¼.
21873-2, 21874-0 Two volumes, Paperbound $6.00

FLATLAND: A ROMANCE OF MANY DIMENSIONS, E. A. Abbott. Classic of science-fiction explores ramifications of life in a two-dimensional world, and what happens when a three-dimensional being intrudes. Amusing reading, but also use-ful as introduction to thought about hyperspace. Introduction by Banesh Hoffmann. 16 illustrations. xx + 103pp. 20001-9 Paperbound $1.00

POEMS OF ANNE BRADSTREET, edited with an introduction by Robert Hutchinson. A new selection of poems by America's first poet and perhaps the first significant woman poet in the English language. 48 poems display her development in works of considerable variety—love poems, domestic poems, religious meditations, formal elegies, "quaternions," etc. Notes, bibliography. viii + 222pp.

22160-1 Paperbound $2.00

THREE GOTHIC NOVELS: THE CASTLE OF OTRANTO BY HORACE WALPOLE; VATHEK BY WILLIAM BECKFORD; THE VAMPYRE BY JOHN POLIDORI, WITH FRAGMENT OF A NOVEL BY LORD BYRON, edited by E. F. Bleiler. The first Gothic novel, by Walpole; the finest Oriental tale in English, by Beckford; powerful Romantic supernatural story in versions by Polidori and Byron. All extremely important in history of literature; all still exciting, packed with supernatural thrills, ghosts, haunted castles, magic, etc. xl + 291pp.

21232-7 Paperbound $2.00

THE BEST TALES OF HOFFMANN, E. T. A. Hoffmann. 10 of Hoffmann's most important stories, in modern re-editings of standard translations: Nutcracker and the King of Mice, Signor Formica, Automata, The Sandman, Rath Krespel, The Golden Flowerpot, Master Martin the Cooper, The Mines of Falun, The King's Betrothed, A New Year's Eve Adventure. 7 illustrations by Hoffmann. Edited by E. F. Bleiler. xxxix + 419pp.

21793-0 Paperbound $2.50

GHOST AND HORROR STORIES OF AMBROSE BIERCE, Ambrose Bierce. 23 strikingly modern stories of the horrors latent in the human mind: The Eyes of the Panther, The Damned Thing, An Occurrence at Owl Creek Bridge, An Inhabitant of Carcosa, etc., plus the dream-essay, Visions of the Night. Edited by E. F. Bleiler. xxii + 199pp.

20767-6 Paperbound $1.50

BEST GHOST STORIES OF J. S. LeFANU, J. Sheridan LeFanu. Finest stories by Victorian master often considered greatest supernatural writer of all. Carmilla, Green Tea, The Haunted Baronet, The Familiar, and 12 others. Most never before available in the U. S. A. Edited by E. F. Bleiler. 8 illustrations from Victorian publications. xvii + 467pp.

20415-4 Paperbound $3.00

THE TIME STREAM, THE GREATEST ADVENTURE, AND THE PURPLE SAPPHIRE—THREE SCIENCE FICTION NOVELS, John Taine (Eric Temple Bell). Great American mathematician was also foremost science fiction novelist of the 1920's. The Time Stream, one of all-time classics, uses concepts of circular time; The Greatest Adventure, incredibly ancient biological experiments from Antarctica threaten to escape; The Purple Sapphire, superscience, lost races in Central Tibet, survivors of the Great Race. 4 illustrations by Frank R. Paul. v + 532pp.

21180-0 Paperbound $3.00

SEVEN SCIENCE FICTION NOVELS, H. G. Wells. The standard collection of the great novels. Complete, unabridged. First Men in the Moon, Island of Dr. Moreau, War of the Worlds, Food of the Gods, Invisible Man, Time Machine, In the Days of the Comet. Not only science fiction fans, but every educated person owes it to himself to read these novels. 1015pp.

20264-X Clothbound $5.00

CATALOGUE OF DOVER BOOKS

LAST AND FIRST MEN AND STAR MAKER, TWO SCIENCE FICTION NOVELS, Olaf Stapledon. Greatest future histories in science fiction. In the first, human intelligence is the "hero," through strange paths of evolution, interplanetary invasions, incredible technologies, near extinctions and reemergences. Star Maker describes the quest of a band of star rovers for intelligence itself, through time and space: weird inhuman civilizations, crustacean minds, symbiotic worlds, etc. Complete, unabridged. v + 438pp.   21962-3 Paperbound $2.50

THREE PROPHETIC NOVELS, H. G. WELLS. Stages of a consistently planned future for mankind. *When the Sleeper Wakes,* and *A Story of the Days to Come,* anticipate *Brave New World* and *1984,* in the 21st Century; *The Time Machine,* only complete version in print, shows farther future and the end of mankind. All show Wells's greatest gifts as storyteller and novelist. Edited by E. F. Bleiler. x + 335pp.   (USO) 20605-X Paperbound $2.25

THE DEVIL'S DICTIONARY, Ambrose Bierce. America's own Oscar Wilde—Ambrose Bierce—offers his barbed iconoclastic wisdom in over 1,000 definitions hailed by H. L. Mencken as "some of the most gorgeous witticisms in the English language." 145pp.   20487-1 Paperbound $1.25

MAX AND MORITZ, Wilhelm Busch. Great children's classic, father of comic strip, of two bad boys, Max and Moritz. Also Ker and Plunk (Plisch und Plumm), Cat and Mouse, Deceitful Henry, Ice-Peter, The Boy and the Pipe, and five other pieces. Original German, with English translation. Edited by H. Arthur Klein; translations by various hands and H. Arthur Klein. vi + 216pp.
20181-3 Paperbound $2.00

PIGS IS PIGS AND OTHER FAVORITES, Ellis Parker Butler. The title story is one of the best humor short stories, as Mike Flannery obfuscates biology and English. Also included, That Pup of Murchison's, The Great American Pie Company, and Perkins of Portland. 14 illustrations. v + 109pp.   21532-6 Paperbound $1.00

THE PETERKIN PAPERS, Lucretia P. Hale. It takes genius to be as stupidly mad as the Peterkins, as they decide to become wise, celebrate the "Fourth," keep a cow, and otherwise strain the resources of the Lady from Philadelphia. Basic book of American humor. 153 illustrations. 219pp.   20794-3 Paperbound $1.50

PERRAULT'S FAIRY TALES, translated by A. E. Johnson and S. R. Littlewood, with 34 full-page illustrations by Gustave Doré. All the original Perrault stories—Cinderella, Sleeping Beauty, Bluebeard, Little Red Riding Hood, Puss in Boots, Tom Thumb, etc.—with their witty verse morals and the magnificent illustrations of Doré. One of the five or six great books of European fairy tales. viii + 117pp. 8⅛ x 11.   22311-6 Paperbound $2.00

OLD HUNGARIAN FAIRY TALES, Baroness Orczy. Favorites translated and adapted by author of the *Scarlet Pimpernel.* Eight fairy tales include "The Suitors of Princess Fire-Fly," "The Twin Hunchbacks," "Mr. Cuttlefish's Love Story," and "The Enchanted Cat." This little volume of magic and adventure will captivate children as it has for generations. 90 drawings by Montagu Barstow. 96pp.
(USO) 22293-4 Paperbound $1.95

THE RED FAIRY BOOK, Andrew Lang. Lang's color fairy books have long been children's favorites. This volume includes Rapunzel, Jack and the Bean-stalk and 35 other stories, familiar and unfamiliar. 4 plates, 93 illustrations x + 367pp.
21673-X Paperbound $2.50

THE BLUE FAIRY BOOK, Andrew Lang. Lang's tales come from all countries and all times. Here are 37 tales from Grimm, the Arabian Nights, Greek Mythology, and other fascinating sources. 8 plates, 130 illustrations. xi + 390pp.
21437-0 Paperbound $2.50

HOUSEHOLD STORIES BY THE BROTHERS GRIMM. Classic English-language edition of the well-known tales — Rumpelstiltskin, Snow White, Hansel and Gretel, The Twelve Brothers, Faithful John, Rapunzel, Tom Thumb (52 stories in all). Translated into simple, straightforward English by Lucy Crane. Ornamented with head-pieces, vignettes, elaborate decorative initials and a dozen full-page illustrations by Walter Crane. x + 269pp.
21080-4 Paperbound $2.50

THE MERRY ADVENTURES OF ROBIN HOOD, Howard Pyle. The finest modern versions of the traditional ballads and tales about the great English outlaw. Howard Pyle's complete prose version, with every word, every illustration of the first edition. Do not confuse this facsimile of the original (1883) with modern editions that change text or illustrations. 23 plates plus many page decorations. xxii + 296pp.
22043-5 Paperbound $2.50

THE STORY OF KING ARTHUR AND HIS KNIGHTS, Howard Pyle. The finest children's version of the life of King Arthur; brilliantly retold by Pyle, with 48 of his most imaginative illustrations. xviii + 313pp. 6⅛ x 9¼.
21445-1 Paperbound $2.50

THE WONDERFUL WIZARD OF OZ, L. Frank Baum. America's finest children's book in facsimile of first edition with all Denslow illustrations in full color. The edition a child should have. Introduction by Martin Gardner. 23 color plates, scores of drawings. iv + 267pp.
20691-2 Paperbound $2.25

THE MARVELOUS LAND OF OZ, L. Frank Baum. The second Oz book, every bit as imaginative as the Wizard. The hero is a boy named Tip, but the Scarecrow and the Tin Woodman are back, as is the Oz magic. 16 color plates, 120 drawings by John R. Neill. 287pp.
20692-0 Paperbound $2.50

THE MAGICAL MONARCH OF MO, L. Frank Baum. Remarkable adventures in a land even stranger than Oz. The best of Baum's books not in the Oz series. 15 color plates and dozens of drawings by Frank Verbeck. xviii + 237pp.
21892-9 Paperbound $2.00

THE BAD CHILD'S BOOK OF BEASTS, MORE BEASTS FOR WORSE CHILDREN, A MORAL ALPHABET, Hilaire Belloc. Three complete humor classics in one volume. Be kind to the frog, and do not call him names . . . and 28 other whimsical animals. Familiar favorites and some not so well known. Illustrated by Basil Blackwell. 156pp.
(USO) 20749-8 Paperbound $1.25

EAST O' THE SUN AND WEST O' THE MOON, George W. Dasent. Considered the best of all translations of these Norwegian folk tales, this collection has been enjoyed by generations of children (and folklorists too). Includes True and Untrue, Why the Sea is Salt, East O' the Sun and West O' the Moon, Why the Bear is Stumpy-Tailed, Boots and the Troll, The Cock and the Hen, Rich Peter the Pedlar, and 52 more. The only edition with all 59 tales. 77 illustrations by Erik Werenskiold and Theodor Kittelsen. xv + 418pp. 22521-6 Paperbound $3.00

GOOPS AND HOW TO BE THEM, Gelett Burgess. Classic of tongue-in-cheek humor, masquerading as etiquette book. 87 verses, twice as many cartoons, show mischievous Goops as they demonstrate to children virtues of table manners, neatness, courtesy, etc. Favorite for generations. viii + 88pp. 6½ x 9¼. 22233-0 Paperbound $1.25

ALICE'S ADVENTURES UNDER GROUND, Lewis Carroll. The first version, quite different from the final *Alice in Wonderland*, printed out by Carroll himself with his own illustrations. Complete facsimile of the "million dollar" manuscript Carroll gave to Alice Liddell in 1864. Introduction by Martin Gardner. viii + 96pp. Title and dedication pages in color. 21482-6 Paperbound $1.25

THE BROWNIES, THEIR BOOK, Palmer Cox. Small as mice, cunning as foxes, exuberant and full of mischief, the Brownies go to the zoo, toy shop, seashore, circus, etc., in 24 verse adventures and 266 illustrations. Long a favorite, since their first appearance in St. Nicholas Magazine. xi + 144pp. 6⅝ x 9¼. 21265-3 Paperbound $1.75

SONGS OF CHILDHOOD, Walter De La Mare. Published (under the pseudonym Walter Ramal) when De La Mare was only 29, this charming collection has long been a favorite children's book. A facsimile of the first edition in paper, the 47 poems capture the simplicity of the nursery rhyme and the ballad, including such lyrics as I Met Eve, Tartary, The Silver Penny. vii + 106pp. 21972-0 Paperbound $1.25

THE COMPLETE NONSENSE OF EDWARD LEAR, Edward Lear. The finest 19th-century humorist-cartoonist in full: all nonsense limericks, zany alphabets, Owl and Pussycat, songs, nonsense botany, and more than 500 illustrations by Lear himself. Edited by Holbrook Jackson. xxix + 287pp. (USO) 20167-8 Paperbound $2.00

BILLY WHISKERS: THE AUTOBIOGRAPHY OF A GOAT, Frances Trego Montgomery. A favorite of children since the early 20th century, here are the escapades of that rambunctious, irresistible and mischievous goat—Billy Whiskers. Much in the spirit of *Peck's Bad Boy,* this is a book that children never tire of reading or hearing. All the original familiar illustrations by W. H. Fry are included: 6 color plates, 18 black and white drawings. 159pp. 22345-0 Paperbound $2.00

MOTHER GOOSE MELODIES. Faithful republication of the fabulously rare Munroe and Francis "copyright 1833" Boston edition—the most important Mother Goose collection, usually referred to as the "original." Familiar rhymes plus many rare ones, with wonderful old woodcut illustrations. Edited by E. F. Bleiler. 128pp. 4½ x 6⅜. 22577-1 Paperbound $1.25

CATALOGUE OF DOVER BOOKS

TWO LITTLE SAVAGES; BEING THE ADVENTURES OF TWO BOYS WHO LIVED AS INDIANS AND WHAT THEY LEARNED, Ernest Thompson Seton. Great classic of nature and boyhood provides a vast range of woodlore in most palatable form, a genuinely entertaining story. Two farm boys build a teepee in woods and live in it for a month, working out Indian solutions to living problems, star lore, birds and animals, plants, etc. 293 illustrations. vii + 286pp.

20985-7 Paperbound $2.50

PETER PIPER'S PRACTICAL PRINCIPLES OF PLAIN & PERFECT PRONUNCIATION. Alliterative jingles and tongue-twisters of surprising charm, that made their first appearance in America about 1830. Republished in full with the spirited woodcut illustrations from this earliest American edition. 32pp. 4½ x 6⅜.

22560-7 Paperbound $1.00

SCIENCE EXPERIMENTS AND AMUSEMENTS FOR CHILDREN, Charles Vivian. 73 easy experiments, requiring only materials found at home or easily available, such as candles, coins, steel wool, etc.; illustrate basic phenomena like vacuum, simple chemical reaction, etc. All safe. Modern, well-planned. Formerly *Science Games for Children.* 102 photos, numerous drawings. 96pp. 6⅛ x 9¼.

21856-2 Paperbound $1.25

AN INTRODUCTION TO CHESS MOVES AND TACTICS SIMPLY EXPLAINED, Leonard Barden. Informal intermediate introduction, quite strong in explaining reasons for moves. Covers basic material, tactics, important openings, traps, positional play in middle game, end game. Attempts to isolate patterns and recurrent configurations. Formerly *Chess.* 58 figures. 102pp.   (USO) 21210-6 Paperbound $1.25

LASKER'S MANUAL OF CHESS, Dr. Emanuel Lasker. Lasker was not only one of the five great World Champions, he was also one of the ablest expositors, theorists, and analysts. In many ways, his Manual, permeated with his philosophy of battle, filled with keen insights, is one of the greatest works ever written on chess. Filled with analyzed games by the great players. A single-volume library that will profit almost any chess player, beginner or master. 308 diagrams. xli x 349pp.

20640-8 Paperbound $2.75

THE MASTER BOOK OF MATHEMATICAL RECREATIONS, Fred Schuh. In opinion of many the finest work ever prepared on mathematical puzzles, stunts, recreations; exhaustively thorough explanations of mathematics involved, analysis of effects, citation of puzzles and games. Mathematics involved is elementary. Translated by F. Göbel. 194 figures. xxiv + 430pp.   22134-2 Paperbound $3.00

MATHEMATICS, MAGIC AND MYSTERY, Martin Gardner. Puzzle editor for Scientific American explains mathematics behind various mystifying tricks: card tricks, stage "mind reading," coin and match tricks, counting out games, geometric dissections, etc. Probability sets, theory of numbers clearly explained. Also provides more than 400 tricks, guaranteed to work, that you can do. 135 illustrations. xii + 176pp.

20338-2 Paperbound $1.50

CATALOGUE OF DOVER BOOKS

MATHEMATICAL PUZZLES FOR BEGINNERS AND ENTHUSIASTS, Geoffrey Mott-Smith. 189 puzzles from easy to difficult—involving arithmetic, logic, algebra, properties of digits, probability, etc.—for enjoyment and mental stimulus. Explanation of mathematical principles behind the puzzles. 135 illustrations. viii + 248pp.
20198-8 Paperbound $1.75

PAPER FOLDING FOR BEGINNERS, William D. Murray and Francis J. Rigney. Easiest book on the market, clearest instructions on making interesting, beautiful origami. Sail boats, cups, roosters, frogs that move legs, bonbon boxes, standing birds, etc. 40 projects; more than 275 diagrams and photographs. 94pp.
20713-7 Paperbound $1.00

TRICKS AND GAMES ON THE POOL TABLE, Fred Herrmann. 79 tricks and games— some solitaires, some for two or more players, some competitive games—to entertain you between formal games. Mystifying shots and throws, unusual caroms, tricks involving such props as cork, coins, a hat, etc. Formerly *Fun on the Pool Table*. 77 figures. 95pp.
21814-7 Paperbound $1.00

HAND SHADOWS TO BE THROWN UPON THE WALL: A SERIES OF NOVEL AND AMUSING FIGURES FORMED BY THE HAND, Henry Bursill. Delightful picturebook from great-grandfather's day shows how to make 18 different hand shadows: a bird that flies, duck that quacks, dog that wags his tail, camel, goose, deer, boy, turtle, etc. Only book of its sort. vi + 33pp. 6½ x 9¼. 21779-5 Paperbound $1.00

WHITTLING AND WOODCARVING, E. J. Tangerman. 18th printing of best book on market. "If you can cut a potato you can carve" toys and puzzles, chains, chessmen, caricatures, masks, frames, woodcut blocks, surface patterns, much more. Information on tools, woods, techniques. Also goes into serious wood sculpture from Middle Ages to present, East and West. 464 photos, figures. x + 293pp.
20965-2 Paperbound $2.00

HISTORY OF PHILOSOPHY, Julián Marias. Possibly the clearest, most easily followed, best planned, most useful one-volume history of philosophy on the market; neither skimpy nor overfull. Full details on system of every major philosopher and dozens of less important thinkers from pre-Socratics up to Existentialism and later. Strong on many European figures usually omitted. Has gone through dozens of editions in Europe. 1966 edition, translated by Stanley Appelbaum and Clarence Strowbridge. xviii + 505pp. 21739-6 Paperbound $3.00

YOGA: A SCIENTIFIC EVALUATION, Kovoor T. Behanan. Scientific but non-technical study of physiological results of yoga exercises; done under auspices of Yale U. Relations to Indian thought, to psychoanalysis, etc. 16 photos. xxiii + 270pp.
20505-3 Paperbound $2.50

Prices subject to change without notice.
Available at your book dealer or write for free catalogue to Dept. GI, Dover Publications, Inc., 180 Varick St., N. Y., N. Y. 10014. Dover publishes more than 150 books each year on science, elementary and advanced mathematics, biology, music, art, literary history, social sciences and other areas.